BEYOND PEDIGREES

Organizing and Enhancing Your Work

Beverly DeLong Whitaker

Ancestry®

Salt Lake City, Utah

929.1
W57b
1993

Library of Congress
Catalog Card Number
93-21029

ISBN Number 0-916489-52-3

First Printing 1993
10 9 8 7 6 5 4 3

For other fine products available from Ancestry, call or write:
ANCESTRY®
Box 476
Salt Lake City, UT 84110-0476
1-800-ANCESTRY
(1-800-262-3787)

This book is dedicated
to my family—
past,
present,
and future.

TABLE OF CONTENTS

LIST OF CHARTS

PREFACE

Genealogists agree that charts of names, dates, places, and relationships form the basis of their family records. Yet most will admit that such a data collection by itself is dry. About all one can tell from a chart showing only names plus birth, marriage, and death dates is that . . .

> they had their kids
>> awfully young,
>>> awfully old,
>>>> or awfully early!

My approach to genealogy is to go *Beyond Pedigrees*, searching for information which can help me visualize what life was like for my ancestors. The chronology of their life events interests me, especially as compared to historical and geographical settings and political events. I want to know how they were influenced by their occupations, religion, educational opportunities, and ethnic background. I enjoy the legends that have been passed down through oral tradition. I treasure written records, family heirlooms, and photo images. And I find satisfaction in locating public records which mark the community involvement of my family.

In *Beyond Pedigrees* I show how to use conventional genealogical materials in unconventional ways. This approach leads to intimate ancestral portraits.

For Whom is This Book Written?

In *Beyond Pedigrees*, I address the hobbyist who fits genealogy into an already busy lifestyle.

I have yet to meet a genealogist who has all the ingredients for a perfect heritage quest—sufficient time, endless energy, ample storage space, vast knowledge, and unlimited funds. The frustrations which accompany limitations cause some people to give up in defeat while others postpone their search until one or more of the difficulties can be totally resolved. Another group remains—and I count myself among them—those who make the most out of every opportunity!

You probably chose to read this book because you already have an assortment of information on your ancestral lines. Now you are confronting a couple of problems. Recognizing the need to organize your material and document your resources, you have acquired and used some basic charts, but you aren't sure what to do next. Or you may feel like you are at a dead end, in need of something to get you moving again.

Genealogical research ought to be fun. It should also be steady, and it requires some structure. In between research trips to archives, courthouses, and libraries, you can do an incredible amount of work in your own home—and at little cost.

For the computer user, I recommend special applications which make use of ordinary word processing, data base, spreadsheet, and graphics software. As an alternative, there are some excellent genealogical software packages to consider.

I find success and satisfaction by applying a mix of creativity, organization, and curiosity to my genealogical pursuits. A logical next step is to share my methods with others. In so doing, I hasten to suggest to my readers that I don't expect anyone to copy my entire approach. Rather, I would encourage you to experiment and adapt since it is this creative process which triggers insight, motivation, and purposeful effort.

How then will this book be different from others in a genealogical reference collection?

First, there are some things it won't cover. It won't provide mailing addresses, descriptions of libraries and archives, legal explanations, nor will it present regional and historical background. But it will tell you why these things are important, how to use such information, and what can be gained by altering perspective. I am suggesting a process that goes beyond pedigrees in order to permit a sense of acquaintance with one's ancestors.

Beyond Pedigrees outlines procedures which can result in fresh perspective, incentive for additional research, and the development of satisfying ancestral sketches. This book outlines a process by which one can organize, analyze, and visualize one's heritage search.

Is There a "Right" Way to Read This Book?

It isn't necessary for you to read straight through this book. However, chapter 1 would be a good starting place since it provides a brief overview of many topics. After that, you can read the chapters in any order. Choose one or two topics that concern you. Give attention to the samples and recommended forms. Begin immediately to use the ideas and techniques, applying them to *two* of your family surnames simultaneously. If possible, choose two families in close geographical proximity but not necessarily in the same time frame.

Work on several projects at one time, alternating between them according to your mood and interests. Take several forms to a copy center and order a supply to keep on hand for periodic use when updating your files. Send out queries and letters and while waiting for responses, go ahead and work on journal or photo collections, a newspaper clipping file, diary entries, or add to a glossary of vocabulary terms. Give attention to a bibliography list and systematically gain access to these books, adding to your own library those which you need frequently for reference. Analyze and summarize those all-important census records. It won't take long to begin a list of your immigrant ancestors, and you can take pleasure in watching the list grow as you identify them. Similarly, you will want to list your ancestors' military connections and occupations. Gradually, you can assemble a research kit or perhaps one for travel and another for home use.

Unleash your own creativity. Design some additional genealogical tools of your own; and share them with others. Don't delay! Your ancestors are out there just waiting to be claimed!

CHAPTER 1

WHAT'S MISSING FROM MY GENEALOGICAL TOOLKIT?

Over a fifteen-year period of doing genealogical research, I concluded that a toolkit of research aids would be valuable. I even purchased sets of forms and books of advice for beginners but found them disappointingly incomplete. Gradually I developed my own methods and forms to make my research efforts more productive. These innovations help me organize to make the most of my research.

In this introductory chapter, I invite you to take note of specific items in my "genealogical toolkit." To make these items more memorable, I've applied alphabetical identification labels to the contents of my special toolkit. Ask yourself how you can use each of the twenty-six aids; are you misusing or neglecting these tools? Do you know how to use these items to the greatest advantage?

I suggest you view this chapter as a teaser. Most of the research aids mentioned here will be covered in more detail in subsequent chapters. However, I recommend that you return occasionally to this summary listing to make sure you don't overlook an essential tool for successful and satisfying genealogical research.

A: Ahnentafel—prepare this as a quick reference to your pedigree.

Ahnentafel is a German word meaning "ancestral table." You can easily produce an indexed list of all your ancestors by using the ahnentafel numbering system, which assigns each ancestor a unique identification number, moving backward in time. You (or the subject of a pedigree) are assigned number 1, your father 2, your mother 3, your paternal grandfather 4, your paternal grandmother 5, your maternal grandfather 6, your maternal grandmother 7, etc. Note that the male is always assigned an even number. Identify the father by doubling an ancestor's number; add one to that number to identify the mother. By listing all numbers sequentially, you prepare an index to your entire pedigree. I draw a line at the break of each generation. Computer users can use one of several genealogy software packages that will compose an ahnentafel from the data you key in. (Chapter 3)

B: Bibliography—make a personalized list of genealogical resources.

In addition to the title, author, publisher, and date of publication for each applicable source, you will want to record the place(s) where each book is available to you either for research or purchase. Moreover, you will benefit by making separate lists for various categories: surnames, geographical locations, histories, etc. Computer users can take advantage of database software to allow easy sorts by category.

C: Census summaries—use these invaluable overviews often.

Providing your original study of a census was thorough, you won't want to repeat your efforts. For this reason alone, it is wise to keep a census checklist; but beyond that, you need to be able to see the gaps in your census work. Until you've confirmed the residence of your ancestor in a specific state and county, you could be wasting valuable effort searching for him in the wrong location. Census work is tedious, time consuming—and vastly rewarding. Although you will discover errors and inconsistencies, there is still much to be gained. Age discrepancies will be frustrating, as will the unexpected spellings and missing children. To resolve some of these matters, maintain a summary sheet for each family; on this sheet, data taken from each census is recorded side by side. These sheets are most fruitful for intensive study, and they are essential take-alongs for day trips.

D: Diary—record your own life events.

Perhaps our best glimpses into the past have been through the pages of diaries such as were kept by the pioneers heading westward. You may have heard it said that today is tomorrow's yesterday. Future generations will know you by what you leave behind in the form of possessions and legends, but you can also share your thoughts with your descendants if you take the time to write them down. Although a diary is usually considered to be a daily or weekly record, it can also be written on a less regular basis and can even focus on a particular subject at each writing. Entries should be dated, and the place of writing should also be recorded. The most interesting diaries combine a description of events with thoughtful reflections about them.

History is made up of *his*-story and *her*-story repeated millions of times with variations both great and small. So be sure *your* story is recorded for a permanent place in history, and remember—the commonplace is frequently as interesting as the unusual.

E: Expense record—list expenses; estimate costs of research plans.

The expense record can be incorporated into a correspondence calendar or maintained as a separate record. Make it only as elaborate as will satisfy your needs. If you are doing research for other people, this effort will require complete accuracy and considerable detail. But perhaps you only want to record how much you paid for a book or for professional research, or the amount you spent on international coupons, SASE enclosures, photocopying, etc. For this purpose you need only record the item and the date, amount, and person to whom payment was made. A budget for research travel is a good idea, and you may wish to list anticipated expenditures to help you prioritize your purchases.

F: Filing system—choose a system and follow it conscientiously.

Your carefully gleaned material is of little use unless you can access it easily and accurately. How sad it is to hear stories of family material that was abandoned or destroyed because no one but the owner could make sense of it. To be realistic about your efforts, consider this time budget: for every hour of research "in the field," match it with an hour at home organizing the material.

There are many excellent books and computer software programs available to help you select or modify a filing system. Even if you don't have a personal computer, you will benefit by thinking about how you could index your files for ready access by a computer; anything stored in computer files must be highly systematic in order to facilitate retrieval. (Chapter 3)

G: Generation charts and family group sheets—enter basic information.

The keystones of genealogy are (1) names, (2) dates, (3) places, and (4) relationships. Add to these elements (5) events and (6) occupations. Reorder the first letters of each of these words and you have the word PONDER, which is exactly what you should do when you are reviewing the information on these charts. None of these facts stands alone; they are interrelated. You need to ponder this information, questioning and seeking new clues. It's at this stage that you are most likely to detect errors or gain new insights. Jot down these thoughts; let your questions form the basis of a brief written plan for confirming your research. (Chapter 3)

H: Heraldic arms—collect these for the fun of it.

It is unlikely that you can prove proper ownership of a heraldic coat of arms. Nevertheless, heraldry holds a fascination for most of us, and there is pleasure to be gained by studying and collecting the crests associated with the surnames in your lineage. Spend time studying books on the subject so that you understand the development and significance of heraldry; be aware of the symbolism, the colors, and the pageantry involved. If you choose to display a heraldic coat of arms, consider grouping several instead of featuring your surname alone, as if you had exlusive right to it. (Chapter 7)

I: Immigrant ancestor list—see how many you can identify!

With the listing of each newly documented immigrant ancestor, you are marking a significant step in your research progress. On this list or chart you need your ancestor's full name, birth and death years, date of immigration, name of ship, place of emigration, and place of immigration. This consolidated listing will prove to be a valuable quick reference whenever you are doing library or archival research. Without it, you are likely to overlook information about an ancestor that may be available in the same indexes you are checking in connection with another ancestor. Moreover, it will be easy to spot incomplete information if you do your list in chart form; seeing a blank area reminds you to do further research on that problem. (Chapter 2)

J: Journal—preserve the family stories.

Although you may have gathered and even systematically and carefully recorded and documented many family names, dates, places, and relationships, you ought to do one more thing. Learning about the associated family legends and traditions is what makes genealogy such an interesting and popular hobby. By assembling bits and pieces of information, you can sketch a word-picture of an ancestor or a specific family and lineage. You might accompany such biographical sketches with descriptions of the geographical surroundings and the political environment, the ancestor or family's problems and accomplishments, and the activities and customs of the day. In a journal, you have the opportunity also to editorialize, making comments about what you think of the facts and stories you have gathered. Remember to indicate the sources of your information. (Chapter 7)

K: Kit—gather your research materials.

Start by making a list of the items to include in a genealogical day-trip bag. Consider what special additions you might need for specific visits. For example, you ought to have some chalk, cornstarch, or flour with you to rub into tombstone inscriptions when you go to a cemetery. (When an inscription is difficult to read, you will find it helps to lighten it using any of the materials suggested above; this technique improves legibility without damaging the tombstone.) Your photo albums and a large, foldable chart should accompany you and your tape recorder and camera to family reunions. A soft cushion and a jacket can add to your comfort at seminars and workshops. Assemble the office supplies you need for your home workspace. Prepare a budget for items you may wish to add such as a small tape recorder or a laptop computer. (Chapter 3)

L : Letters—keep up a steady correspondence.

Get into the habit of writing many genealogy letters. Often you will find that one correspondent leads to another, or that you exchange letters with certain persons over and over for years. You may even decide to arrange a personal meeting or at least add a telephone or computer modem interchange of information. One of the greatest benefits of correspondence will be the friends you make.

Initially, your letters should be very brief, and they should focus on only one or two questions or pieces of information. Except when writing to governmental bodies, include an SASE each time you initiate correspondence; subsequent letters to the same person do not require an SASE. Be sure also to keep copies of the letters you send out so that you understand the answers!

M: Migration maps—explore genealogical geography at its best!

Map study is fascinating, particularly when the area relates to your own heritage. Acquire period maps whenever possible. You may have the good fortune to locate a county map with your ancestor's name inscribed as a landowner. Possibly you'll acquire a plat map along with a deed. Boundary line changes are significant to census study. Historical maps will show county and state boundaries and may also include battle sites, railroad lines, and migration trails. By using such maps and comparing them to a list of your family's chronological residences, you can prepare your own family migration maps. Use one color for a father's surname and another for the mother's, tracing their geographical genealogy back from the point where they met; add a legend that includes dates and cities or counties. You will be surprised at how much insight you gain from this exercise. (Chapter 5)

N: Newspapers—assemble a clipping collection.

The first item we think of from the newspaper is an obituary. Obituaries often contain much that is interesting and useful to the genealogist, though errors surface if the data was provided to the newspaper by someone who had incomplete or inaccurate information. Birth and marriage announcements may also be located, and legal notices can prove valuable. Actual news coverage about an ancestor is particularly welcome. But even if you don't have that good fortune, it will be worth your time to read the local newspaper on microfilm for the place and period where your ancestors were living. You will acquire the flavor of their lifestyle, become acquainted with their neighbors, and even capture some of the subjects of their thoughts. (Chapter 4)

O: Occupation descriptions—imagine your ancestors' daily lives.

How fortunate you are if you are able, through censuses, diaries, letters, family legends, or even photos, to determine the occupation of an ancestor. If you are, go a step further and research the occupation as it was lived in that location and in that period of time. What tools and dress were required? What status, rewards, problems, attitudes, opportunities were associated with the profession? Who else in the area shared a common occupation? What training or education was required and how was it achieved?

P: Photograph album—preserve a visual heritage.

Much has been written about photography; the very subject has its own genealogy. Sometimes you can determine the approximate date of a photograph by identifying what type of photograph it is. Learn, too, about proper restoration and preservation of photos, and acquire acid-free storage for them. Give creative thought to their display. Consider acquiring copies or at least make photocopies to place in a travel album that you can carry without risk of losing or damaging originals. Provide copies for other members of the family; include proper identification on the back in pencil. Complete identification includes the name of the person(s) shown, the date and place of the photograph, and a lineage chart to show the relationship of the photographed person(s) to yourself or to the person to whom you are giving the photo. Karen Frisch-Ripley's *Unlocking the Secrets in Old Photographs* (Ancestry 1991) can help you solve the mysteries contained in family photographs. (Chapter 7)

Q: Queries—prepare and send these to genealogical publications.

One of the chief advantages of belonging to a genealogical society is the opportunity to submit query letters. Most societies have guidelines to follow in terms of length, abbreviations, etc. Study the queries that appear in the publication to which you are sending yours, and pattern yours after them. The most successful queries set the stage for answers by providing two connected names with their relationship specified, a specific setting, and a specific time period. Request specific and limited information. Keep copies of your queries and record them on your correspondence calendar. Acknowledge and retain the answers you receive, even if they have provided little assistance—what appears at first to be useless may later prove to be a connection. Don't overlook the value of responding to queries yourself. Your information may be just what the other person needs, and it may lead to benefits for you as well. (Chapter 6)

R: Recordings—capture your family on tape.

Both audio and video recording are within the technological and economic means of many families. Nothing comes closer to capturing the spirit of a family than being able to see and hear a live account of a shared heritage. Taping also provides an opportunity to involve other persons in your immediate family by engaging them in the technological and interpersonal aspects of the project. Computer technology is already available to allow digitized photos and tape-recorded sounds to be incorporated into on-screen slide shows. At the very least, you'll want to gain proficiency in handling live audio interviews for later transcription. There are many excellent books that can help you prepare for a taping experience

S: States—learn unique features of states key to your research.

You can learn much to enhance your understanding of your family if you take the time to get acquainted with the history and geography of the states in which they lived. This is particularly true for the early years of our country and further back into colonial days: borders changed, mountains and rivers influenced settlements, religious and ethnic influences were significant, political attachments were powerful, occupations meshed with the surroundings, and strong personalities left their mark. There is much to learn about the contrasting legal practices from state to state. If most of your research centers in a few states, you will want to assemble your own handbook for research in those states. Look to the excellent books that are available on specific states for guidance.

T: Timelines—pinpoint important events in your ancestors' lives.

You will be surprised at how helpful it can be to make a chronology of an ancestor's life events. Marking them on a timeline covering that person's lifespan graphically shows the gaps in information about the individual. You might want to include historical events on the timeline in order to consider what the impact may have been on that life. It is helpful to record the person's age next to each major event. If you include the birth dates and birthplaces of the person's children, you have hints about when moves took place. Likewise, you can record the location of the person or family at each census. A timeline becomes a marvelous study tool, providing you with data to evaluate from a different perspective. (Chapter 4)

U: "Uni-forms"—design forms to use at archives and courthouses.

Publishers have made available a wide variety of forms, and you can supplement them by creating templates for your own specific needs. You can save time and become more efficient with your research if you use "uni-forms" to extract information from probate papers, land deeds, court cases, census records, tombstones, and military matters. In the rush of trying to accomplish much in a short amount of time, it is easy to forget to record significant details, but a well-designed form serves as a timely reminder. Later, in analyzing the data, uniformity helps put statements into perspective. (Chapter 2)

V: Vocabulary list—acquire a glossary of genealogical terms.

You will encounter unfamiliar words in your research; for example, some special terms appear in religious records, particularly among the Quakers, and every occupation has its own vocabulary. In addition to a written definition of each term, you may want to show its pronunciation and origin. Many of these words are of a legal nature and most are still in modern usage, though some are archaic. You may also need a foreign language dictionary. Books giving the origins of names can be interesting and useful. Build an alphabetical glossary either by filecard or with computer software. Alphabetical sorts may be done rapidly by computer. If you use filecards, punch a hole in the corner of each one and string them together on a keychain so they stay in order. *Ancestry's Concise Genealogical Dictionary* (Ancestry 1989), by Maurine and Glen Harris, is a quick-reference source created specifically for genealogists.

W: War charts—compare dates and ancestral involvement.

You will probably want more than one kind of war chart. One could be a list of ancestors who had military service; it should include rank, unit, and dates of service. Perhaps you would benefit from a composite list of wars and their dates, with which you can compare the life spans of specific ancestors to assess their possible involvement either as soldiers or as affected citizens. You may also need a sequential list of battles for a specific war so that you can compare dates and places with the same type of information concerning your ancestors.

X: Extra copies—share your research.

Eventually you may choose to publish a book about one or more of your families. Meanwhile, be generous in exchanging information with your network of family researchers. Photocopies are fairly inexpensive, and computerized information can be transmitted by modem, fax, exchange of floppy disks, or printouts. Include your name, address, phone number, the date, and documentation of the source of the information you are sharing. Often, what you send is forwarded to someone else, who in turn may establish a correspondence with you and even be able to provide you with additional material. On your correspondence calendar, indicate what you have provided, again with the date. (Chapter 8)

Y: Yearly events—know the historical settings for your pedigree.

No man or woman has lived apart from his area's history. To know what an ancestor's life was like, you need to know what was going on in that person's world. Acquire or produce your own corresponding extended calendar of events. There are excellent books, charts, and computer software packages that detail yearly events in a variety of fields—political, cultural, scientific achievement, etc. Computer users can easily extract the portion that parallels the lifespan of a particular ancestor; similarly, you can photocopy portions of printed lists. Living family members are usually quite interested in the events that occurred during their own birth years. Such information can even be incorporated into biographical sketches. (Chapter 4)

Z: Zero-in plan—develop a plan of "next steps" for researching.

Each time you review your progress with a particular surname, you need to zero-in on your next research steps. Identify problems, anticipated results, and possible sources of information. One of the best ways to prepare thoroughly is to divide a summary sheet into two columns. Label the left column "fact" and label the right one "opinion." Based on the known, identified, written-out facts, suggest and write possible directions and sources to be checked out. These are temporary worksheets that need to be revised and rewritten as research continues.

CHAPTER 2

AM I FOLLOWING APPROPRIATE RESEARCH PROCEDURES?

- Courtesy, persistence, documentation.
- Contents of a travel bag for genealogical day trips.
- How to prepare a surname list that will quickly show others the names being researched along with regions and time periods.
- Category listings: religious and organizational affiliations, immigrants, veterans, places of residence, etc.
- Brief mention of various kinds of records available for research—family, public, church, etc.
- Forms for abstracting information from public records.
- Census data forms and checklists.
- Research logs and correspondence calendars, address files.
- Value of a descriptive reference list of libraries and archives.
- Purpose of keeping bibliographies by both surname and region.
- A checklist for evaluating research progress.
- Suggestions for making analysis planning sheets for future research.
- A flowchart of genealogical research steps.

As you associate with other persons engaged in genealogical research, you discover there are certain procedures accepted as standard. Yet you hear excuses:

"My records are a mess."

" I can't tell you the source because I didn't write it down."

"I forgot that I had already read that census."

"I'm not sure, but I think I used this book before."

"I prepared a list of books to check today but left it home."

"I wrote to a lady in either Nebraska or Nevada but haven't had an answer yet."

In this chapter I only hint at the vast resources available and the methods for successful access. I strongly recommend that you read several books on how to do genealogical research. Pay particular attention to chapters that tell you in detail how to search courthouse records and other public and private record depositories.

The researcher in any field of study sometimes finds it tedious to keep detailed reference records. However, the time spent in documentation pays off dramatically and marks the difference between credibility and confusion. This chapter suggests a variety of forms you can use to systematize the records of your research progress.

Guidelines: Courtesy, Persistence, Documentation

If "rules" or "commandments" appear too stringent, at least let us consider some guidelines for genealogists. "Courtesy" is a broad term that might be extended to include foresight, consideration, kindness, appreciation, thoughtfulness, honesty, and perhaps, under certain circumstances, even sympathy or forgiveness. It is, of course, inexcusable for a person to deface or remove archival or printed material. Rudeness, sarcasm, harsh criticism, and inconsiderate behavior create problems for persons associated in any way with the offender. Go out of your way to show appreciation to persons who help you. Don't be stingy or insincere with your compliments. Remember your manners!

A good genealogist is also a persistent genealogist. Since one is never finished, it should go without saying that one must never give up! One of the premises of this book is that reexamination of the data you've collected will always hold potential for a new breakthrough.

Document! Without documentation, your research is only hearsay. If you want people to believe you, you are going to have to show proof that your information is accurate. Cite your sources; label your materials; cross-reference with codes (see chapter 3).

Travel Bag for Genealogical Day Trips

If you are like most genealogists, you welcome all opportunities to visit libraries and archives, courthouses and cemeteries, workshops and society meetings. But do you go prepared? My slogan is, "Have bag, will travel!" In truth, I really do keep a tote bag partially packed and ready to go. I store a clipboard of notebook paper and a folder of basic forms in a side pocket, along with a plastic-covered surname list, as described later in this chapter. Two lightweight notebook binders stay in this bag, too. One is my travel collection of family group sheets; the other is my personalized "research handbook." This handbook includes a slim atlas, a small map collection, my research calendar, a short glossary of terms, my census checklist, a bibliography of needed books, some timelines, and any special listings I've prepared. In a small zipper bag, I keep a container of dimes and quarters for parking and the photocopier, a battery-lighted magnifier, pencils and pens, erasers, address labels, a pad of self-sticking memos, and a few file cards. Sometimes at the last minute I add one or two temporary colored research folders of specially prepared material in expectation of doing work in a particular geographical area or on specific surnames. If you prefer a businesslike appearance, use a briefcase reserved exclusively for genealogy work.

Surname List

Be prepared to exchange information. The next time you are at a library or genealogical group meeting and someone asks you what names you are researching, show them a list of names instead of merely answering with one or two names. By listing only the odd numbers in the ahnentafel numbering system (chapter 1), you can create a list of all your surnames. Such a list can be alphabetized in seconds if you type them on a computer using software that does alphabetical sorts. A column for dates and another for places of residence makes this list even more valuable. Slip the list into a brightly colored plastic see-through binder, and lay it on top of your notebook and papers to catch the eyes of other researchers. This same list makes a valuable checklist for you to use when you are checking through several pages of queries in the genealogical publications. Even though your mind is focused on a few surnames, you may be rewarded by spotting information related to one of the other names on your list.

Surname List

Surname	Early Area, Years	Recent Area, Years

Kinds of Records Available for Research

As you pursue your heritage, you will want to seek information from as many kinds of records as possible. Begin your research by consulting with members of your immediate family. Tape record and transcribe interviews whenever possible. Look through family artifacts and memorabilia. Make photocopies of written material.

Public records are of great variety. One expects to find marriage, death, probate, land, and military records; but there are also guardianships, lawsuits, tax lists, voting records, jury service rosters, and immigration papers.

Church records may include christenings, membership transfers, records of service, and memorials. Marriages were usually recorded by a minister in his own book, which only rarely has survived. Sometimes marriages, births, and deaths were also recorded in minute books or other official church logs. Quaker records even report many complete families.

Cemetery custodians kept plats and lists of burials. Large cemeteries may have these available for research. Across the country, much effort has been made by historical and genealogical societies to copy tombstones and publish them in books, newsletters, and other publications.

Newspapers published legal notices of probates, auctions and sales, divorces, bankruptcies, court claims, and convictions. News items included births, marriages, deaths, obituaries, anniversaries, advertisements, visitor lists, and local news.

Abstract Forms for Public Records

When you enter a courthouse, be prepared! Do your homework so that you know what to seek. This is one of the times you can benefit by using a temporary surname research folder. At the very least, you would want copies of your family sheets since collateral lines are likely to appear as neighbors in the public records.

Give some advance thought to how you will record any information you find in public records. Take uniformly sized lined paper with you (preferably 8½" by 11") and copy or abstract each record on a separate sheet; include the date and place of abstraction.

Census Forms

It would be difficult to overestimate the value of census study as a basis for pursuing an American lineage. Census data is available in other countries as well, although the format will be a little different.

Because census work is both time consuming and basic, it is best tackled in

Census Checklist

Surname: _____

County & State Searched	1790	1800	1810	1820	1830	1840	1850	1860	1870	1880	1900	1910	1920

a methodical manner. It is widely known that, for most states, American census data is available at ten-year intervals beginning in 1790, except for most of the 1890 census. Prior to 1850, the only given name to appear was that of the head of the household, although sex and age categories are represented. Beginning in 1850, censustakers were required to record individual names and ages plus certain other data. The information gathered varied from one census to another; the data was entered in tabular form and is best transcribed by using table forms which match the record for that year. Such forms are available through publishers and at some libraries and genealogical societies; use them! The forms will remind you to include the date, location, residence number, microfilm roll number, and other important information.

It helps to consolidate census data for a particular family on one summary sheet; then it becomes easy to trace moves, occupations, and expanding families. By comparing the names of children, it is possible to follow the family even after a father's death. This type of sheet is a good one to include in one's temporary surname research folder. Forms for this purpose can be purchased, or you can design your own.

In briefer form, some people like to use a checksheet that lists which censuses have been checked, the code number where the record is filed, and a statement as to whether results were negative or positive. Census checksheets, one per surname, can be placed as an addendum to the research log. I've included such a chart for your use.

Research Log

My research log is composed of separate sheets for each surname (multiple sheets as they become necessary) filed alphabetically. For uniformity and ease of use, I prepared a form and had it duplicated. I keep the log in my research handbook along with a few maps, lists, and references that pertain to my specific research tasks. This notebook goes with me on all library and courthouse trips. Frequently, a quick check of my research log prevents me from repeating research in a book I have used previously.

Entries in a research log ought to be brief. A reference to material acquired at a library should give the surname; the date of the research; the name and city of the library; the title, author, and call number of the book; page number and subject matter; and finally the File Folder Code (e.g., GA,0023). Courthouse information would follow a similar pattern.

Correspondence Calendar

A correspondence calendar will help you keep track of your correspondence. Use the form I provide, another standard form, or make use of a computerized

Research Log

Date	Library & Call No.	Title & Author	Comments/Page No.	Filing Code
Surname:				

Correspondence Calendar

Date	Correspondent	SASE	$	File Code	Surname

template. If you produce your form on a spreadsheet, you can maintain a running total of your correspondence expenses. Or you might prefer to use a database for sorting purposes. Integrated software that allows conversion from one application to another makes it possible for you to achieve both purposes. Some people like to include the address here as well, but I prefer to keep a separate address list rather than copy it.

Address File

You can either keep an address file as a list or in an address book. Computer users have a distinct advantage here: by placing addresses in a database, it is easy to do sorts or searches or to alphabetize; you can also print out labels, address envelopes, or insert addresses into form letters through mail merge. I have a preference for being able to identify all my correspondents associated with a particular surname. You may find it useful to have a list for courthouses or one for libraries, annotated not only with phone number but also the hours they are open for service and the name of a contact person.

Libraries and Archives

Plan to maintain an up-to-date list of the libraries and archives in your area. In addition to address and telephone number, note the hours; directions on how to get there and where to park; the name of a contact person; and any special collections, charges, or other unusual features. Gradually add information for more-distant libraries, including those operated by lineage or genealogical societies, historical organizations, and religious groups. Compile a list of governmental archives at both state and federal levels. Even if you have few opportunities to visit in person, you can effectively use the mails with little expense beyond postage.

Bibliographies

As you begin to establish your own personal booklist, examine the bibliographies listed in major genealogical reference books. Newer and reprinted volumes will show up in publications and catalogs. Read and ponder the reviews in publications. Transfer appealing titles to your own list, possibly using computer database software. In addition to the usual bibliographical data, allow space for a notation as to where a copy of the book is located for your access. Indicate where the book can be purchased; but when you find the book in a library,

List of Libraries and Archives

Name & Address	Phone/Hours/ Contact Person	Special Collections	Special fees & Misc.

Bibliography for Genealogy Research

Subject	Title	Author	Pages	Cost	Source

record that location as well. An alphabetical listing by author or title is of less value than one that groups books by subject. Two major subject categories, "Surnames" and "Region," could be subdivided. Additional subject areas might include such topics as "Civil War," "Revolutionary War," "Map Sources," "Immigration," "How-to Books," and "General Reference."

If you use a personal computer to establish and revise your booklist, it is easy to sort by subjects and print updated versions frequently. If you compose your bibliography by hand or on a typewriter, make separate sheets for each category, then add to each sheet. Keep your bibliography sheets in a research handbook to carry with you on research trips. During any library visit, take time to compare your list with the card file and make note of any books included in their collection. Before subsequent visits to libraries, you will be able to consult your bibliography and incorporate those books into a research plan merging availability of resources with specific quests.

Category Lists

There are several more lists you'll want to develop. Start out with a regional list. Add lists of immigrant ancestors, migrations, military service, yearly events and occupations, vocabulary glossary, and war charts. Brief listings by category encourage you to do further topical research without overlooking persons or events that have commonality apart from their relationships. Inevitably, the very process of composing these lists will provide you with innumerable research possibilities, many of which you have previously overlooked.

Checklist for Evaluation

Unless your research is limited to one or two surnames, you need a method to evaluate and chart your research progress. It's easy to overlook resources or to assume you've already checked something when you really haven't. Consider making copies of my checklists, or design your own. Use one for an individual or for each ancestral couple, compiling them into family units by surname. Mark the individual's identification number for easy cross-reference along with name, years of birth and death, and spouse's name. Plan to use this in connection with the matching family group sheet or, as an alternative, have the checklist form printed on the back side of your family group form. When you are focusing attention on an individual and other generations of the same family, examine accompanying checklists to see what research activities ought to be undertaken. These checklists can be placed into temporary, colored pocket folders labeled with the surname; add an analysis planning sheet or a flowchart along with timelines and pertinent data about the family which you might need for reference away from home. With such preparation, research trips or family

Family History Checklist for
Completed Searches

Name of ancestor(s):

Census	Where?
_____	1790 _____
_____	1800 _____
_____	1810 _____
_____	1820 _____
_____	1830 _____
_____	1840 _____
_____	1850 _____
_____	1860 _____
_____	1870 _____
_____	1880 _____
_____	1890 _____
_____	1900 _____
_____	1910 _____
_____	1920 _____
_____	State census: _____
_____	State census: _____

Vital	Where?
_____	Birth _____
_____	Marriage _____
_____	Death _____

Family

_____ Bibles
_____ Legal Papers
_____ Journals, diaries
_____ Letters
_____ School, church
_____ Photographs
_____ Heirlooms
_____ Medical
_____ Military
_____ Farm/business
_____ Genealogies
_____ Pedigree Charts
_____ Insurance
_____ DAR, SAR

Land

_____ Deeds, abstracts
_____ Mortgages
_____ Grants, patents
_____ Surveys, maps

Probate

_____ Wills
_____ Administrations
_____ Inventories
_____ Packets
_____ Guardianships

Community

_____ Church
_____ Mortuary
_____ Cemetery
_____ Fraternal
_____ Occupational
_____ Newspaper
_____ Orphanage
_____ School records
_____ Voting lists
_____ County histories

Public Notices

_____ Divorce notices
_____ Court records
_____ Tax lists
_____ Passenger lists
_____ Passports
_____ Naturalizations
_____ Legal notices
_____ Bank notices

Military

_____ Service records
_____ Pension

Ancestor Checkpoints

Name of ancestor:

___ Birth date	___ Illnesses
___ Birthplace	___ Travel
___ Father	___ Organizations
___ Mother	___ Landowner
___ Spouse	___ Religion
___ Marriage date	___ Education
___ Marriage place	___ Political leanings
___ Other marriages	___ Court appearances
___ Children	___ Occupation
___ Death date	___ Military service
___ Death place	___ Pension
___ Place of burial	___ Residences
___ Physical appearance	

interviews have multiple and clear goals, and quests are more likely to be successful.

If you know all of the details listed above, you will have a fairly complete profile of your ancestor. This list of checkpoints is composed of the pieces essential to a biographical puzzle portrait. Each piece is unique, yet they interlock. When you assemble a jigsaw puzzle, you begin to get an idea of what the completed picture might look like even before it is complete. However, you aren't completely satisfied until all of the pieces fit together.

Analysis Sheets

Depending on the nature of your research problem, one or more analysis sheets can clarify problems. In addition to the checklists mentioned above and the timelines described in chapter 4, I make either a *fact/opinion chart* or a *concept map* for each research problem. I add this to a temporary surname research folder and take it with me on trips.

Fact/opinion Chart
The fact/opinion chart might also be referred to as a T-chart. The top of the T is a line on which to record the name and identification number of a particular ancestor. A perpendicular line splits the page into one side for *facts* and one

Fact/Opinion Chart

Ancestor: ID No.:

Facts	Opinions

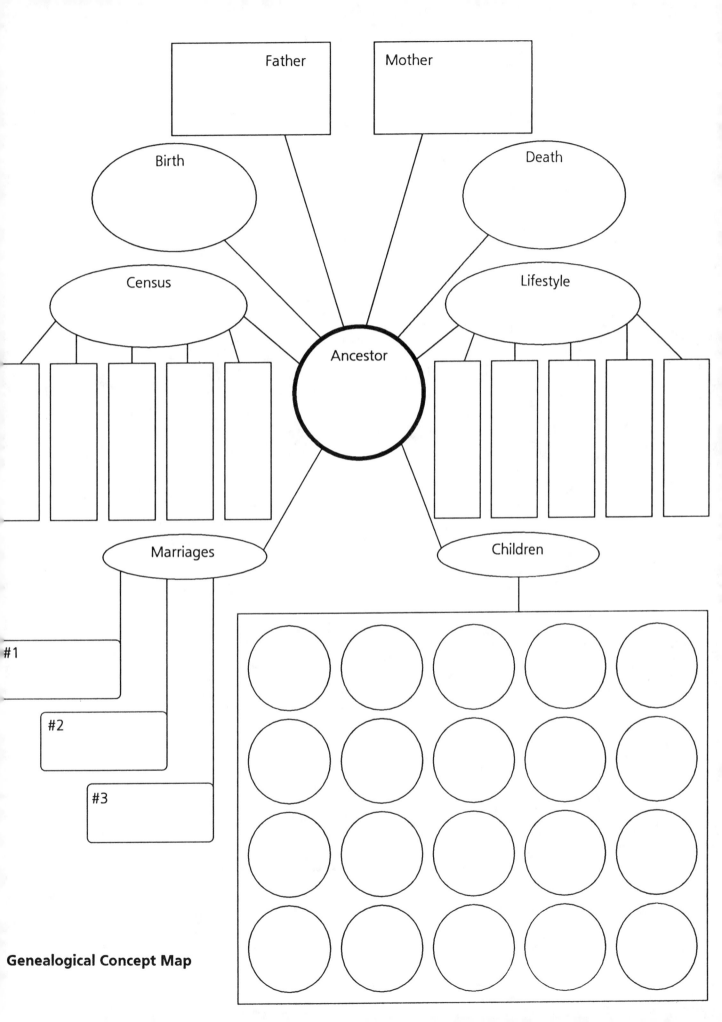

Genealogical Concept Map

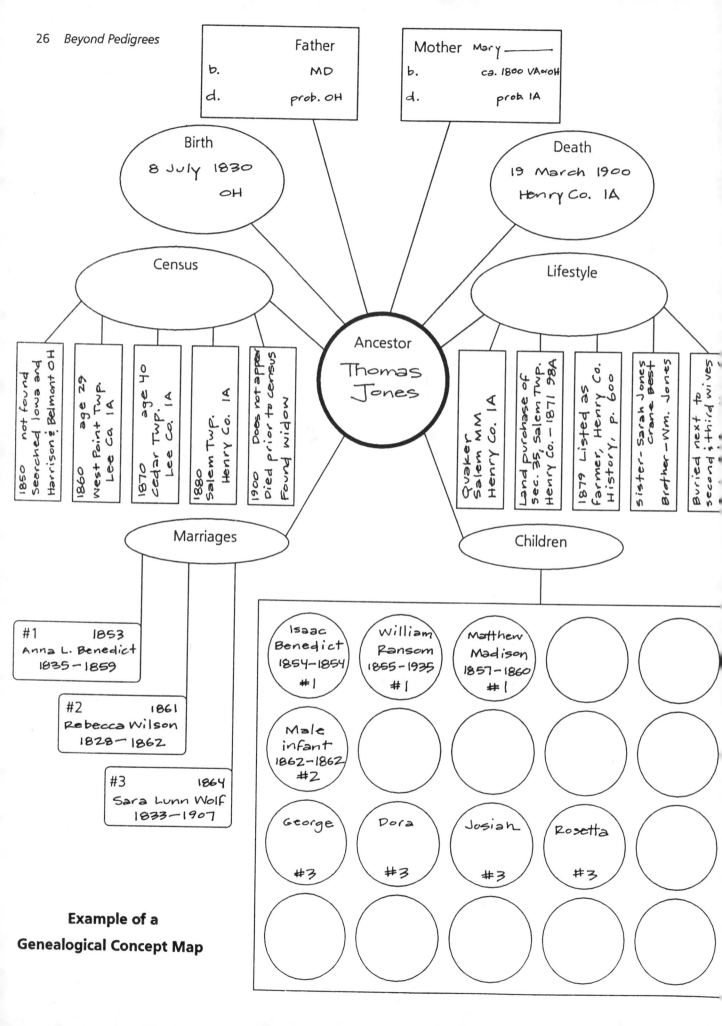

Father
b.   MD
d.   prob. OH

Mother Mary ————→
b.   ca. 1800 VA or OH
d.   prob. IA

Birth
8 July 1830
OH

Death
19 March 1900
Henry Co. IA

Census

1850   not found
Searched Iowa and
Harrison & Belmont OH

1860   age 29
West Point Twp.
Lee Co. IA

1870   age 40
Cedar Twp.
Lee Co. IA

1880
Salem Twp.
Henry Co. IA

1900 Does not appear
Died prior to census
Found widow

Ancestor
Thomas Jones

Lifestyle

Quaker
Salem MM
Henry Co. IA

Land purchase of
Sec. 35, Salem Twp.
Henry Co. — 1871 98A

1879 Listed as
Farmer, Henry Co.
History, P. 600

Sister – Sarah Jones
Crane Best
Brother – Wm. Jones

Buried next to
second & third wives

Marriages

#1   1853
Anna L. Benedict
1835 – 1859

#2   1861
Rebecca Wilson
1828 – 1862

#3   1864
Sara Lunn Wolf
1833 – 1907

Children

Isaac Benedict
1854 – 1854
#1

William Ransom
1855 – 1935
#1

Matthew Madison
1857 – 1860
#1

Male infant
1862 – 1862
#2

George
#3

Dora
#3

Josiah
#3

Rosetta
#3

**Example of a
Genealogical Concept Map**

side for *opinions* which derive from the parallel facts. Listing facts chronologically will be easier if you've already prepared a timeline for the ancestor; or you could develop the two projects simultaneously.

Concept Map

The concept map is a visual representation, a method used extensively as a study skill for content reading and test preparation in academic disciplines. It consists of circles, rectangles, and lines connecting significant data in a meaningful way. The idea here is to focus on one main idea and up to seven supporting details. Seven is something of a "magic" number for short-term memory. It's a way to learn essential information; it's also a way to make a clear presentation of material to someone else. Information for the concept map comes largely from a family group sheet. Nongenealogists seem to find family group sheets dull. By contrast, a concept map stirs curiosity, and appeals particularly to persons who prefer visuals to words.

A Flowchart of Research Steps

Persons who have done some computer programming or who have studied computer logic may find it appealing to organize their research steps into a flowchart pattern. This logical process presents an almost uncanny parallel to genealogical problem-solving; that is because computer technology imitates human brain function. Computers are able to reach a decision point and branch off, then return, continue, and so on. The brain can do this and more; the brain has the extra capacity to look simultaneously at the whole as well as the parts. Yet we tend to limit our own brainpower, often by expending our energy on details out of context from the whole. One value of a flowchart is that it provides a pattern that systematizes the problem-solving process; another is that it makes a powerful visual impact.

Flowchart of Research Steps

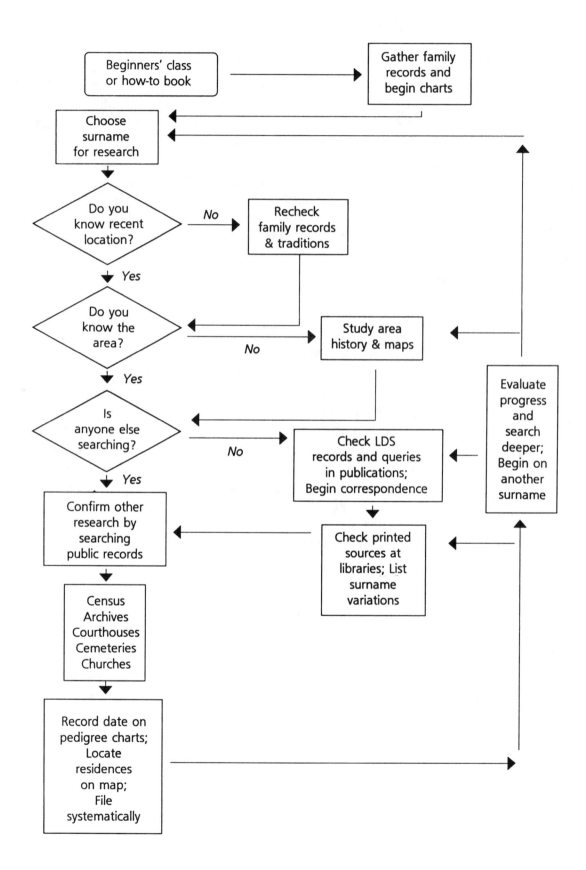

CHAPTER 3

CAN I FIND WHAT I'VE FILED AWAY?

- Organizing a workspace in your home for genealogical work.
- Reference books and materials.
- Logic for dividing research results into either four or eight sections (grandparent or great-grandparent surnames).
- Basic pedigree charts in common usage.
- Use of "fan" charts as a visual index.
- Preparation of generational grids.
- Options for filing—folders, binders, computer disk storage.
- Documentation; indexing systems.
- Computerized database for efficient search and cluster functions.

Any hobby requires both space and supplies, and certainly genealogy is no exception. At minimum, you need a supply of basic pedigree charts, family group sheets, and a workable system for viewing them.

Computerized records offer distinct advantages to the family researcher. If you have a computer, examine and compare the commercial software programs available to keep track of an extended family. I use commercial genealogy software and supplement when necessary with templates of my own design, using business software.

In this chapter I suggest a number of options for filing materials in a home office setting. Do yourself the favor of developing a filing system instead of a dumping area.

Study this chapter and then make up a list of essential supplies to purchase. To further clarify your thinking, write a brief summary of your chosen filing system. Could someone else enter your genealogical corner and make sense of your records? If not, why not?

Organizing a Workspace

The successful genealogist is likely to be a person who likes an orderly life. Genealogy as a hobby does take considerable space because it involves growing amounts of paper, books, and artifacts. There are stages in this hobby that you must recognize. At first you probably had just a few documents, a typed manuscript or family history book, and some old pictures and letters. Soon you may have added several court records, photocopies and notes from library visits, a few reference books, a photo album, and considerable correspondence. Seeing the need to organize this material, you branched out with file folders and/or binders and probably provided yourself with access to a typewriter or personal computer. A few of my friends have devoted entire rooms to the pursuit of genealogy; one of them even parked a small trailer-house on her lot, dedicated solely to this interest! But most of us have to be satisfied with a corner in a room shared with other members of the family and a variety of activities. Here are some suggestions for maximizing your workspace:

1. Find space for a file cabinet with some drawers for your exclusive use.
   Alternative: portable plastic or metal fileboxes and cardboard storage boxes.

2. Add a set of bookshelves.
   Alternative: bookends or small individual book racks.

3. Acquire a desk or sturdy table with good lighting.
   Alternative: a folding table and a small desk lamp.

4. Try to obtain both a typewriter and a personal computer and printer.
   Alternative: a large supply of good ballpoint pens, quality paper and carbon paper, trips to a photocopier, a hired typist.

5. Use a bulletin board, folding screen, or wall area for large charts, maps, and items of genealogical interest.
   Alternative: Be creative and mount charts on the backsides of hanging pictures, hiding them from public display but keeping them where you can easily find them. Transform family artifacts into art objects and create a display of ancestral portraits.

6. Organize appropriate office supplies—including a stapler, staple remover, paper clips, rubber bands, three-hole punch, one-hole punch, gummed hole reinforcements, memo pads, self-stick removable notepads, file cards, file dividers, three-ring binders, acid-free storage materials, computer supplies, disk storage boxes, typewriter ribbons, correction fluid, stamps, address labels, bookmarks, file folders, self-sticking labels, scissors, newspaper clipper, ruler, erasers, tape, carbon paper, letter opener, magnifying glass, pencil sharpener,

postage scale, tape recorder and cassette tapes, pocket calculator, a perpetual calendar and a current calendar, stationery, a supply of 8 ½"-by-11" lined notebook paper, typing paper, envelopes of various sizes, mailing labels and, of course, a variety of pens and pencils. You might even add a paper cutter, hanging files for your filing cabinet, and other conveniences.
Alternative: Start with the basic necessities, shared with other members of the household. But begin immediately to gather your own supplies. Perhaps you can place them in a carry-all container that can be tucked out of sight when not in use but can still give you easy access to all the items you might need.

7. Consider adding such things as your own photocopier, a microfiche or microfilm reader, a modem for your computer, and even a fax machine.
Alternative: Be glad you have use of your telephone! And allow time and money in your budget to make trips near and far.

Reference Books and Materials

As you improve your work area, you will find the desire to do an increasing amount of your genealogical work from this "home base." Gradually you will build a collection of reference books and other printed materials. Keep these in your work area rather than on shelves or boxes in another room. Have a place for storing periodicals, catalogs, newsletters, and special mailings.

In a file drawer or similar-size storage box separate from your family files, store folders pertaining to the methodology of genealogy. I recommend a folder for each state and country where you research. This is the place for you to reclaim your how-to clippings and lecture notes pertaining to specific geographical locations. Also store supplies of favorite forms and outline maps. File those monthly society newsletters. Add a folder for heraldry, one for lineage societies, another for a specific religious group, perhaps one on photography and preservation. Use a black felt-tip pen to label your file folders, and you will find it easy to spot the correct file quickly. Within categories (for example, states), alphabetize the files for easy retrieval.

Inevitably you will have overlapping material to cross-reference. And you may choose to place certain material in binders, at least when you are taking them away from home.

Dividing the Research Collection

Early in my research efforts, I recognized that I could have a problem keeping my families straight. How easy it is, for example, to confuse persons from one grandmother's line with those in the other grandmother's pedigree! I reduced that confusion by dividing my notebook of family group sheets into four sections: one for each grandparent. Then, in a second notebook, I did the same for my husband's family. In assigning the ahnentafel numbers, I began with our children, assigning number 2 to my husband and number 3 to myself. By doubling the numbers, my in-laws are numbers 4 and 5; my parents are 6 and 7. My husband's grandparents carry the numbers 8, 9, 10, and 11; my grandparents' numbers are 12, 13, 14, and 15.

Eventually I encountered an unusual problem and temporarily assigned two numbers to one ancestor. My great-great-grandparents probably were unaware that they descended from brothers several generations in their past. My bookkeeping task would have been easier if the generation spans had been equal. In great-grandfather's family, however, there were only five generations, whereas there were seven in great-grandmother's until they reached their common ancestor. I designated the male lineage number to continue the line back into the past; this is the family I am able to trace back to the origins of the name in thirteenth-century England, with resulting large ahnentafel numbers for the remote ancestors.

Pedigree And Lineage Charts

A basic tool for genealogists is the *pedigree chart*. There are slight variations, but they share a common format that begins with one individual and traces back three or four generations, always with the father's line above and the female below. There is space to record the dates and places of the significant life events (birth, marriage, death) for each person on the chart. Notebook-size charts (8½" by 11") are readily available; they show either four or five generations. I prefer using four-generation charts, adding new ones for each individual appearing at the fourth generation. As you identify distant ancestors, you will see the value of acquiring an additional, larger chart that shows as many as ten or twelve generations.

The logical and practical supplement to pedigree charts are *family group sheets*, which should be completed for each ancestral pair in a pedigree. When a man has multiple marriages, there should be multiple sheets for him since each of these forms provides space for a wife and her children. Likewise, a woman may have more than one sheet due to remarriage. Again, various publishers make slight variations in what they include on the form, but the purpose of this form is always to provide a summary of one family unit. Perhaps its greatest value is the access it provides to collateral lines of brothers and sisters along with surnames of the same geographical area as identified via the marriages of these children. These open valuable doors to successful research.

You need a large supply of both forms, particularly the latter. Both charts are readily available from any genealogy supplier and also from some libraries and most genealogical societies, or you may use the one I've provided. You may prefer to design your own adapted form and take it to a copyshop for bulk-rate copies. Since you are likely to place them into three-ring binders at some point,

Four Generation Pedigree Chart No. ___

Prepared by _____

Address _____

Phone _____ Date _____

No.1 on this chart is the same person as no.____ on chart no. ____

8. _____ ___
birth
place
marriage
place
death
place

4. _____
birth
place
marriage
place
death
place

9. _____ ___
birth
place
death
place

2. _____
birth
place
marriage
place
death
place

10. _____ ___
birth
place
marriage
place
death
place

5. _____
birth
place
death
place

11. _____ ___
birth
place
death
place

Ancestors of
1. _____
birth
place
marriage
place
death
place

12. _____ ___
birth
place
marriage
place
death
place

6. _____
birth
place
marriage
place
death
place

13. _____ ___
birth
place
death
place

3. _____
birth
place
death
place

14. _____ ___
birth
place
marriage
place
death
place

7. _____
birth
place
death
place

15. _____ ___
birth
place
death
place

Family Group Record

HUSBAND _____ ID# _____
Occupation _____ Church _____
Lived at _____
Military Service _____
Born _____ Place _____
Married _____ Place _____
Died _____ Place _____ Buried at _____
Father _____ Mother _____
Other wives _____

WIFE _____ Occupation _____ Church _____
Lived at _____
Born _____ Place _____
Died _____ Place _____ Buried at _____
Father _____ Mother _____
Other husbands _____

Sex	Child's Given Name	Birth Date/Place	Death Date/Place	Date/Place of First Marriage	Spouse	ID No.
	1					
	2					
	3					
	4					
	5					
	6					
	7					
	8					
	9					
	10					
	11					
	12					

Compiler _____ Date _____
Address _____

I suggest that you have them punched and that you take into consideration the spacing of those holes as you prepare your original.

Ancestor tables for each surname, including the ahnentafel, can be easily prepared from a set of pedigree charts. Lineage charts trace only one line; they can be compiled from either a pedigree or a descendancy. I identify ancestral photos in an album side by side with a lineage chart. Although more than one surname may appear via a mix of male and female ancestors, a lineage represents each generation with only one ancestor, always in the direct line.

A *descendancy* starts with one person far back in time and proceeds with a comprehensive descent list, generation by generation, moving forward in time; these are sometimes referred to as a "genealogy." Several numbering systems are in use and can be seen in printed books entitled *The Descendants of _____*. Modified descendancies are frequently seen in presentations of royal lines.

Relationship charts are used to trace two separate lineages to a common ancestor. These are convenient for establishing the relationship that exists between you and a distantly related correspondent. Relationship charts have been designed quite differently by different authors. You will want to collect a variety and photocopy them to insert in your research handbook.

Fan Charts

I've indicated that four-generation and five-generation pedigree charts are available from many sources to show one's pedigree of direct ancestors, moving backward in time. I use four-generation charts to precede the family group sheets in each section of my travel notebook. Some people like to use folded charts which show as many as fifteen generations. Most show only seven to twelve generations. These large, folded charts make appropriate "take-alongs" for research trips or family reunions. I have a seven-generation wall chart on a bulletin board near my files. This chart, which is nearly complete, attracts much interest from visitors to our family room where I've located my "genealogical corner."

But the easiest way for me to visualize my total ancestry is with four six-generation *fan charts*, one for each of my grandparents. Placed together, they form a large, circular chart composed of six concentric circles made up of one-inch bands. Each grandparent's fan chart is divided into generation levels: 1, 2, 4, 8, 16, and 32—for a total of sixty-three ancestors in each quartile. Each name carries the appropriate ahnentafel number, so it is an index to my entire lineage records. Four of these fan charts, punched and printed on 8½"-by-11" paper, fit into my travel notebook; this helps me to move back and forth from family to family as I research a particular geographical area where families overlap. A similar set of four sheets allows me to work on my husband's lines as well. When I show these two circular sets of fan charts to our children, they are able to see their heritage from the fourth through the ninth generations.

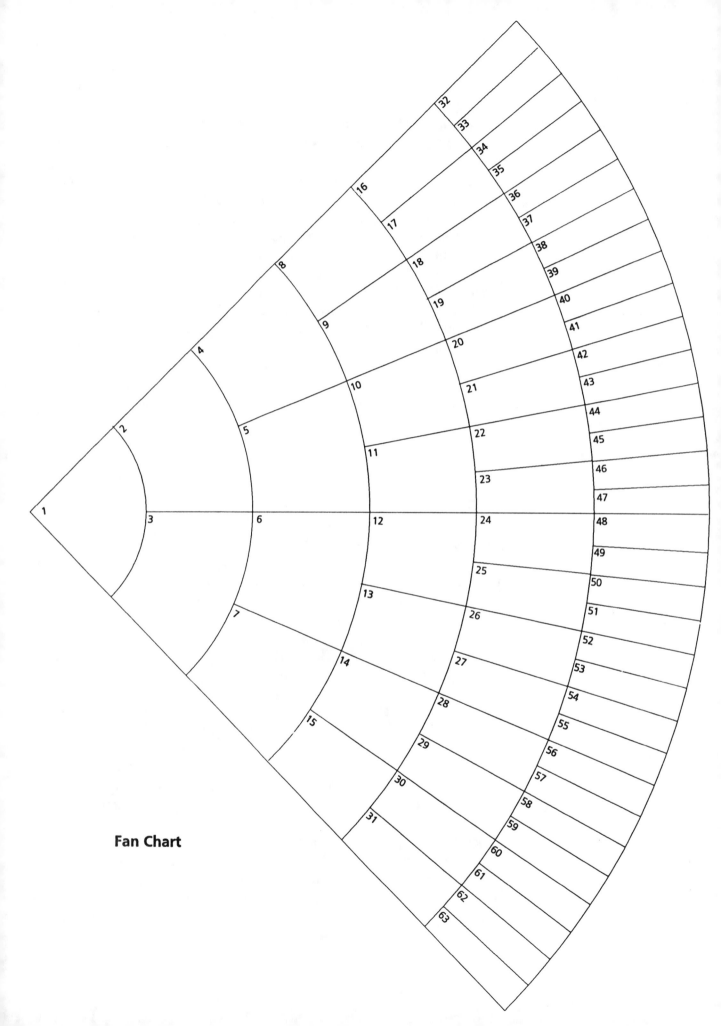

Fan Chart

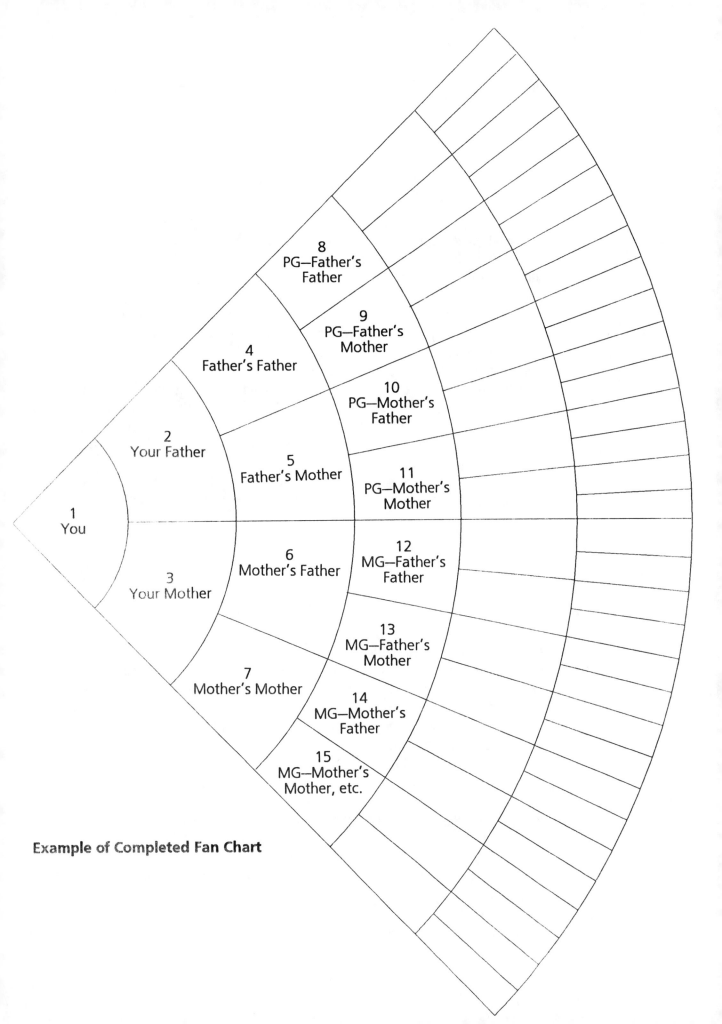

Example of Completed Fan Chart

This is adequate for them since they already know the members of the first three generations.

Generational Grid

You can easily make a six-generation grid on a computer spreadsheet or even on a single sheet of lined notebook paper to identify the generational descent of your first thirty-two surnames. This gives you each surname lineage horizontally. Vertically, you can identify by generations. Divide your paper into six one-inch columns and number vertically from 1 to 32 in the left margin and again in the right margin for easy tracking. Across the top, label the columns A through F. Record yourself at A1, your father at B1, your mother at B17, your paternal grandfather at C1, your maternal grandfather at C17, your maternal grandmother at C25. Continue horizontally to extend the surnames. Now add the wives in column D at 5, 12, 21, and 29. Extend those surnames. Next, add the wives in column E at 3, 7, 11, 15, 19, 23, 27, and 31. Extend those surnames into column F and add the wives into the remaining spaces there. Using regular-sized print and a typewriter or word processor, you can do a similar chart of four generations.

(Note: Using compressed print on a computer printer, you can show six generations. This can be done either in word processing or with an indexed spreadsheet.)

Filing Options

Folders, Binders, or Computer Disk?
Perhaps you have already established a satisfying way to file your materials. Although some people use a card file system, most genealogists follow one of three methods or combinations: file folders, notebook binders, or computer disk storage. Each has advantages and disadvantages; all need to be cross-referenced to their support documents.

A travel notebook of family group sheets is my most useful reference. These are subdivided into eight families (each of the great-grandparents of my children). Alternative and perhaps better ways of organizing this binder would be either alphabetically by surname or numerically by ahnentafel identification numbers. Contained in this one notebook are (1) names, (2) dates, (3) places, and (4) relationships—the four keystones to genealogy. Not to be overlooked are the collateral lines and the marriages into other families—all of which are listed here for ready reference.

I rarely take a file folder of basic documentation to a library or courthouse, partly because I fear losing things, especially loose papers in a file folder. There

Generational Grid

	Generation 1	Generation 2	Generation 3	Generation 4	Generation 5	Generation 6	
	A	B	C	D	E	F	
1							1
2							2
3							3
4							4
5							5
6							6
7							7
8							8
9							9
10							10
11							11
12							12
13							13
14							14
15							15
16							16
17							17
18							18
19							19
20							20
21							21
22							22
23							23
24							24
25							25
26							26
27							27
28							28
29							29
30							30
31							31
32							32

Example of a Completed Generational Grid

	Generation 1	Generation 2	Generation 3	Generation 4	Generation 5	Generation 6	
	A	B	C	D	E	F	
1	Beverly DeLong	R. Newell DeLong	Louis DeLong	Robert DeLang	Leberecht DeLang	?	1
2						?	2
3					Beate Nichols	?	3
4						?	4
5				Pauline Altman	Gottfried Altmann	Johann Altmann	5
6						?	6
7					Augusta Werner	?	7
8						?	8
9			Edna Britton	G.A. Britton	Robert Britton	Thomas Brereton	9
10						Betsy Dobson	10
11					Margaret Anderson	Peter Anderson	11
12						Sarah Matthews	12
13				O. Pearl Williams	J. H. Williams	J. Wesley Williams	13
14						C. Deardoff	14
15					Mary E. Dickey	Samuel Dickey	15
16						Mary E. Mathis	16
17		Velva Thornburg	Charlie Thornburg	Abner Thornburg	H. Thornburgh	Jacob Thornburgh	17
18						Rachel Hammer	18
19					Athalinda Bond	Edward Bond	19
20						Ann Hayworth	20
21				S. Alpha Watton	John D. Watton	David Watton	21
22						Sarah Davis	22
23					Minerva J. Tryer	John Tryer	23
24						Rebecca Walker	24
25			Annetta Jones	William Jones	Thomas Jones	?	25
26						Mary ?	26
27					Anna Benedict	Isaac Benedict	27
28						Rebecca Wing	28
29				Ionia Thompson	C. A. Thompson	S. Thompson	29
30						Jane ?	30
31					Mary James	Henry James	31
32						Ellen ?	32

are times, however, when I plan to travel and research in a specific geographical area and wish to have considerable information with me about one or more families in that area. In preparation for a research trip to an archives or courthouse, I prepare a set of colored pocket/brad folders, one for each surname. I use the brads to hold in place the timelines, lists, etc., which I have prepared as my tools for "research readiness"; the pockets are ready to accept material I acquire at the site. Upon my return home, I am able to continue work on each family, updating my files and records.

At home, on my genealogy bookshelf, I keep eight separate notebook binders, one for each of the great-grandparents. Contained therein are copies of the family group sheets for home reference, supplemented by condensed biographical sketches and timelines.

My filing cabinets hold all my backup source material. Whereas everything in my bookshelf notebooks pertains to proven family, the file folders will include research on various surnames, much of which will eventually prove to be associated with persons unrelated to my family. This "null" research has its value and should not be discarded; it should, however, be annotated when it is known to concern persons outside the family.

Because I have a personal computer, I have considerable information in disk storage. By establishing a data bank of family group sheet material, I can print on the screen or make hard copies of a wide variety of information about specific ancestors or families. In addition, I use the computer to develop forms, lists, indexes, timelines, charts, correspondence, and biographical sketches. Most of these things can also be done with a typewriter or by hand. The primary advantage of a computer is that it can do rapid data sorts of stored material. A second advantage is the ease with which one can copy information to send to correspondents. Increasingly, we are seeing family histories being prepared fairly inexpensively through the use of computer technology.

Documentation and Indexing Systems

Entire books have been written on filing systems. The important word here is "system." Without a clear, consistent, and workable system, your research data will be unintelligible both to you and future generations. The key categories around which to organize your research data are (1) surname and (2) geographical location; some persons separate (3) documents, and (4) correspondence. And when a piece of research is tied to one individual, it is useful to label it with the ahnentafel identification number as well.

When I began my research, I labeled all materials simply by letter and number. The letter I used was the first letter of the surname of my children's eight great-grandparents since, conveniently, there happened to be no duplication of initials! The number was simply sequential according to when I obtained the information. But as my files began to bulge, I realized this system was inadequate. I found myself going through thick folders, subdividing them into the various surnames belonging to each family. This approach gave me excellent perspective of my research problems; I began to see connecting links and clues for additional research.

Finally, I took each of my families and each of my husband's families and gradually reindexed those files into individual surnames with each subdivided geographically. Now, for example, my limited Jones family research, although still contained in one file folder, is subdivided into research gathered in Iowa, Indiana, and Ohio. My migrating Thompson family makes better sense to me now that it is subdivided into Ohio, Illinois, Iowa, Missouri, Kansas, Colorado, Idaho, and general (for a few items not geographically oriented). The Whitaker file folders include one for England and one for Ireland as well as one each for Pennsylvania, North Carolina, Georgia, and several other states. Because of extensive correspondence on this line, there are additional file folders labeled with Whitaker and the name of the correspondent. Similarly, my extensive Thornburg collection occupies a number of file folders, expanded from only one original file folder!

Within each surname's geographical file, I still code each sheet of research data with a sequential number, (e.g., WHITAKER: GA,0023). I use a four-digit number beginning with placeholder zeros in order to accommodate computer indexing and cross-referencing. The entry cited simply indicates that I can find any reference to this document simply by going alphabetically to W in my reference files, finding the collection of Whitaker folders, then going within the Georgia section and locating sheet 23 in numerical sequence. When I pull that sheet, I might find that it pertains to a specific person, in which case an identification number would also appear. Further documentation of the source of information would also appear on this sheet.

Most of the paper in my file folders will be of uniform size since I do all my extraction of data on 8½"-by-11" notebook paper. An oversized document might be kept in an acid-free envelope but would have an index reference sheet in the file folder to indicate where the document is stored and what it is.

It is my practice, when taking research notes, to always record the source location and date on the upper right corner of my paper. I leave room for the indexing code on the upper left, assigning the next sequential number when I place it into the appropriate file folder. At the same time, I place that number on my research log for easy cross-reference. The research log contains only very brief and basic entries, but it provides an invaluable index to one's research effort (see research log, chapter 2).

By documenting all research materials carefully, you are prepared to cross-reference easily and accurately. The code number can appear on a family group sheet as well as on indexes and checklists. This solves the problem when you are asked, "What is your proof?" An annotated family group sheet will make you aware, for example, that a date of death appeared both on the tombstone and in an obituary, or that the place and date of a marriage are based on a copy of the marriage license. Accurate and complete documentation is the mark of a true genealogist.

Using a Computerized Database

An advantage available to computer users is the opportunity to generate reference lists through a well-designed database. Business software can be adapted for this purpose, sometimes more effectively than specific genealogy software. Preplanning is essential; it may be impossible or at least inefficient to open additional fields once the project is underway. After determining the various fields into which you plan to enter information, test your database with a small number of entries and then make appropriate modifications. In the trial run process, be sure to experiment with a variety of data sorts and printouts, including both on-screen prints and hard copy designs. Realize that you will be unable to see all the data on screen at any one time and that planning the sorts becomes the significant issue.

Equally important to the use of the computer for sorts is the use of the database for search. Again, business software is adequate; in fact, you can make use of the same database for certain types of searches as you used for sorts. Both searches and sorts are most helpful when you are able to enter more than one determinant. But by clever maneuvering and comparison of lists, one can get around the problems posed by even limited databases. It takes good planning to maximize your computer's capacity while minimizing the keystrokes of tedious data entry.

Try this set of fields for your computer database:

Suggested Fields for Computer Database

Field Content	No. of Spaces
Surname, given name	25
ID no. (15 spaces allows decimal system for collaterals)	6 to15
Relationship (A=ancestor, C=collateral, U=unknown)	1
Event, year (b=birth, m=marriage, d=death, r=residence)	5
State or country (2 spaces for state or 3 for country)	3
Locale (city and/or country)	15
Record (c=census, l=land, m=military, p=probate, o=other)	1
Index code	6

CHAPTER 4

DO I KNOW HOW TO GO BACK IN TIME?

- How timelines provide insight into the decisions and actions of ancestors.
- Purpose of individual chronological lists for each ancestor.
- Making approximations on ages and dates.
- Peculiarities of the Julian and Gregorian calendars; European-style dating; Quaker-style dating.
- Linkages to historical settings through printed resources.
- Daily life patterns—transportation, occupations, dress, medical treatment, architecture, entertainment, education, religious practices, ethnic traditions.
- Information accessible via newspapers, old letters, legal documents, and published regional histories and genealogies.

Can you picture for yourself what life was like in another era? Whatever effort you put forth to study history will add immeasurably to your comprehension of the influences that shaped your ancestry. History may not have been your favorite subject back in high school or college, but something dramatic occurs to most of us when we insert our own family into the span of years and the events of history.

In this chapter I urge you to develop and study timelines and chronologies. Think about the span of generations in your own family. Enjoy gathering historical data to enrich your comprehension of the daily lives of your ancestors.

I suggest resources for historical information that you should find helpful. Also, you will want to note peculiarities associated with calendars.

Timelines

Our ancestors did not live in a vacuum; their lives were affected by persons and events both close at hand and far away. It is imperative for the genealogist to acquire a sense of time and history. One of the easiest ways to visualize the impact of historical events is to study timelines. You can make use of timelines already published in books, or you can develop your own timelines to correspond with specific periods in history that are of most interest to you.

To construct a timeline yourself, begin by selecting a span of time and subdividing it into equal units. A century, for example, might be divided into ten equal periods. A highly detailed timeline might cover only a year or two. You can plot one with a pencil and ruler, or you can use commercial computer software. Graph makers or even a timeline software package will work, but so will a regular spreadsheet program. Recently, some genealogical publishers have included timeline forms in their catalogs. A timeline that shows the overlap of generations within a lineage would be especially helpful.

Life Spans of the Britton/Brereton Lineage

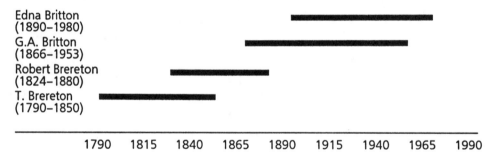

Edna Britton (1890–1980)
G.A. Britton (1866–1953)
Robert Brereton (1824–1880)
T. Brereton (1790–1850)

1790   1815   1840   1865   1890   1915   1940   1965   1990

Chronological Lists of Events

You will benefit by looking systematically and chronologically at the events in the life of an ancestor. Transfer information recorded on family group sheets to a chronology for a single ancestor. Put his name and identification number at the top. Record the date in the first column, the event in the second, the place in the third, and comments and file code in the fourth. Proceed down the page, adding more events, particularly moves to new places of residence. Childhood residences can often be determined from the father's family sheet by noting the birthplaces of brothers and sisters. Likewise, adult residences can be noted based on birthplaces of children. Major life events may be known and recorded, including military service and marriage. Places of death of certain family members may add clues. Items in file folders may provide dates and places for land purchases, tax payments, and church records. Census records will round out the picture. Record the information as you locate it, then rearrange it by chronological order. This is particularly easy to do with a computer using software that allows sorts by sequential numbers; place the year in a field separate from the day and month so that you can sort chronologically by year.

Timeline for Henry James, 1815–post-1885

Year	Event	Location and/or Relationships
1815	Birth	Pennsylvania; reported in census records
1837	Son born	Will, Ohio
1840	Son born	Joseph, Ohio
1840	Census, 20–30	Kirkwood T., Belmont Co., Ohio; 2 boys under 5
1840	Census: father?	John at Hendrysburg, Kirkwood T., Belmont Co., Ohio
1845	Daughter born	Mary E., Belmont Co., Ohio
1846	Daughter born	Martha, Ohio
1848	Son born	Thomas, Ohio
1850	Census, age 35	Kirkwood Township, Belmont Co., Ohio
1850	Son born	Wilson, Ohio
1850	Census: mother	Mary, age 61, born Penn.; living with Henry
1851	Son born	Alex, Ohio
1852	Son born	Robert C., Ohio
1854	Twins born	Charles W. and Ella, Ohio
1859	Daughter born	Lola B., Ohio
1860	Census, age 42	Kirkwood Township, Belmont Co., Ohio
1861	Daughter born	Rosa, b. Ohio; in 1880 census but not 1860
1863	Daughter married	Mary, at Lacon in Marshall Co., Ill.
1865	State census	Not in Lacon Township, Marshall Co., Ill; check more
1870	Census	Not in Marshall Co., Ill.; search Iowa, Co. 9
1880	Census, age 65	Liberty Township, Republic Co., Kans.
1885	Census, age 67	Republic Co., Kans.
1885	Census	Wife still living, age 63, Republic Co., Kans.
1885	Agric. census	Republic Co., Kans. Living with son, Wilson

An individual chronology converted into a proportionately spaced timeline will likely show major gaps in information. Where information is missing or incomplete, you have a starting place for further research. Too often one's research focuses only on the places of birth and death, with so many opportunities missed along the way. Once an ancestral chronology or individual timeline is developed, it can be useful to superimpose it upon a historical timeline. At the very least, this activity will suggest major events that could have shaped a life. Was there a threat of war? Was the area becoming overcrowded? Was cheap land available somewhere else? Was statehood already accomplished? Was the slave issue an influence? Was religious freedom hampered? Was good transportation available?

The computer user can develop one template for chronologies and another for timelines. Depending upon what software is used, columns can be organized by using tabs in a word processor, columns in a spreadsheet, or database printouts. Integrated software may allow transference from one to another according to purpose.

Approximating Ages and Dates

You can assume a generation span of twenty-five to thirty years. If you assume twenty-five years per generation, realize that tracing your family back fifteen generations will involve 32,768 ancestors and will take you back to the sixteenth century. In twenty generations you will pass the million mark with 1,048,576 ancestors. Mention these facts to the people who innocently inquire of you, "Have you finished your genealogy yet?"

You can apply formulas to known information to estimate dates of birth, marriage, and death. Determine a fairly wide span in which to search following the formulas below.

To estimate a male's birth date when marriage date is known:
      Marriage date - 40 years = beginning of years to be searched
      Marriage date - 16 years = ending of years to be searched

To estimate a female's birth date when childrens' birth dates are known:
      Birth date of last child - 50 years = beginning of years to be searched
      Birth date of first child - 16 years = ending of years to be searched

To estimate a marriage date when childrens' birth dates are known:
      Birth date of last child - 35 years = beginning of years to be searched
      Birth date of first child + 1 year = ending of years to be searched

To estimate a death date when birth date is known:
      Last date known alive = beginning of years to be searched
      Birth date + 90 years = ending of years to be searched

Personal Chronology

Date	Event	Location	Comments	File Code

Ancestor: _____ ID No.: _____

Calendars

Are you familiar with the peculiarities of the Julian and Gregorian calendars, European-style dating, and Quaker-style dating?

In 46 B.C. Julius Caesar instituted a new calendar that brought together lunar and solar time—quite an improvement over previous calendars. He determined that the solar year was 365 days and six hours; consequently, his calendar made provisions for an extra day to be added every four years. This Julian calendar was used throughout the Christian world. Caesar's calculations were off by only eleven minutes and fourteen seconds, but by the year 1582, the discrepancy amounted to ten days. Pope Gregory decided to reform the calendar by directing that 4 October 1582 be followed by 15 October, and he also made an adjustment in leap years. This calendar, known as the Gregorian calendar, now prevails, and we are right with the sun. Because Gregory was head of the Roman Catholic church, Catholic countries adopted the new system quickly. England, always in difficulty with the Church of Rome, refused to adopt the new calendar officially until 170 years later, by which time the difference between the Julian calendar and the sun amounted to eleven days, and according to the English government the new year did not begin until 25 March. By this time, in the colonies, many people were beginning to use the Gregorian system. A system of "double dates" resulted, and in early colonial records dates appear like "8 March 1656/57"—the first year representing the Julian calendar, the latter the Gregorian. Sometimes letters were used in recording dates, the letters *O.S.* indicating the old style dating and *N.S.* indicating the new style. In 1752, the English government converted to the Gregorian calendar and also recognized 1 January as New Year's Day. Consequently, double dating is a phenomenon that occurs in colonial records only in the months January, February, and March in or prior to 1752. Surprisingly, China waited until 1912 to adopt the Gregorian calendar; Russia, 1917; Greece, 1923; and Turkey, 1928.

Dates in colonial seventeenth century frequently indicated the month by its number instead of its name, primarily because most of the months had pagan names unacceptable to the Puritans and the Quakers. Generally the day was given first, then the month. In working with old dates, compare enough dates to determine if this holds true. The Quakers, along with everyone else in England and the American colonies, did not begin using the Gregorian calendar until 1752. Consequently, in using the old Quaker records, remember that until 1752 the "1st mo" is March.

As you record dates on charts, follow the accepted genealogical practice of listing the day first, followed by the month abbreviated, and then the full year (4 Jul 1776). If you are a computer user who is designing templates, you should consider splitting dates into two fields: one for the day and month and a second one for the year; this enables you to sort chronologically by year. A sort will not work if the day, month, and year appear in the same field. Planned spacing and the use of tab spacing gives the appearance of one column in printouts. Allow two characters for the day, three for the month, and four for the year, with single spaces in between. When entering a day comprising a single digit, begin with a space or a zero to hold the place.

Obtain a perpetual calendar to keep in your research handbook. I use one that covers the years 1800 through 2050. A miniaturized set of fourteen different calendars takes care of all years, including leap years.

Links to History

As you build your personal reference library, include books that describe the historical settings against which your ancestors' lives were played out. You will want histories for the countries from which your American ancestors originated, and you will need a general American history as well as some regional ones. Add books on specific military and political events. If you like fiction, historical novels are an enjoyable way to gain insight into the lives and times of an era in which a particular ancestor lived.

Movies, television, and videotapes offer a stimulating visual opportunity to explore history. Vintage music is available on records, cassettes, and compact disks. Attend historically-based plays and reenactments whenever possible. You can also join historical societies, subscribe to history magazines, and attend lectures on historical and genealogical subjects.

Visit living museums as well as those displaying archival material. Enjoy opportunities to tour old houses, birthplaces and homes of famous people, battlefields, preservations, and public buildings with a special heritage.

Daily Life Patterns

It has never been enough for me to gather dates and places of my ancestors. I want to know what they were like, what their problems may have been, how they lived their lives. What can be learned about an ancestor's daily life patterns? How were they affected by transportation, occupations, dress, medical treatment, architecture, entertainment, education, religious practices, and ethnic traditions?

Transportation: I like knowing that Robert Brereton arrived from Ireland at New Orleans and came up the Mississippi River on a steamship.

Occupations: I'm proud of a photograph of John Watton in his blacksmith apron, holding the tools of his trade.

Dress: I have a scrap of fabric from a dress that belonged to Sallie Matthews, the great-grandmother of my father's mother. I created a button collage representing five generations on my mother's side.

Medical treatment: Knowing something about the medical treatment practices of an earlier day helps me to appreciate a story about a nineteenth-century pioneer ancestor, Henry James. He had been very ill and in grief, his family had begun to prepare him for burial. His face was nicked as they shaved him and, surprisingly, he moaned! They realized he was still alive, and he recovered and lived many more years; however, because of his superstitious personality and their own state of shock, the family never told him what had happened.

Architecture: I have a description of Athalinda Bond Thornburg's log cabin, and another of the German-style house that Gottfried Altmann built when he arrived in southeast Iowa.

Entertainment: Barn raisings and dances in western Kansas provided Ionia Thompson with entertainment. An 1888 courtship photo of George Britton and Pearl Williams was taken at the county fair. The game of Rook was the delight of families in the village of Lowell, Iowa, early in the twentieth century along with noisy chivarees for the newly-married. (A *chivaree* was a surprise celebration by the couple's friends, who announced their arrival with noisemakers or by beating on pots and pans. Gifts of canned goods and other food stuffs were then presented to the new homemakers.)

Education: Education was important to Louis and Edna DeLong, enough so that Edna and the children lived in town during the week so the children could attend high school, rejoining Louis on the farm for the weekend. Not surprisingly, several of their descendants have been teachers—including me!

Religion: Several religions are identified in my genealogy—Baptist, Methodist, Roman Catholic, Lutheran, Huguenot, Dunkard, and Quaker. My mother's Thornburg surname can be traced back through Quaker records to the religion's origins in the1600s.

Ethnic traditions: Contributing to my heritage, ethnic traditions in my lineage were carried into this country from Germany, France, Poland, Switzerland, Spain, Canada, England, Ireland, Scotland, and probably Wales.

Resources from the Past

You can find some of this type of information via newspapers, old letters, legal documents, and published regional histories and genealogies.

I spent two days (a year apart) reading microfilmed newspapers at the state library in Topeka, Kansas, searching for information about my ancestors who married near Colby and then turned back to Iowa when the rest of the bride's family continued traveling west. On my second visit, I found a tiny news item announcing their marriage in 1889. Previously I had found her sister's marriage and the grades both had earned during their summer Normal training. I also discovered when and where they found employment.

Reading old letters can make you feel as if you are trespassing—yet there were usually good reasons for saving those letters, and they were often kept specifically so that future generations could have them. Recently I came into possession of letters saved by my grandfather. These letters included correspondence between his grandmother and her sister-in-law. At about the same time, through a chain of coincidences, we identified a family photo of this sister-in-law and made the acquaintance of a descendant. I have since met this lovely lady, but first we came to know each other through the telephone and an exchange of correspondence. Imagine how we felt when at last we met and sat together, rereading the letters that had traveled between our two ancestors over one hundred years ago!

Legal documents are curious treasures because of the handwriting flourishes and archaic spellings found in them. Holding a copy of signed citizenship papers, I felt almost like I had stood nearby at the courthouse while great-great-grandfather renounced his loyalty to a monarch in a far land and declared himself an American. I am helping my husband pursue the genealogy of his family's Georgia farm, where my father-in-law spent seventy-nine of his eighty-two Christmases; deeds and plat maps are a part of this search. I have the pension papers of my Illinois Union soldier ancestor, and my husband has his great-grandfather's Confederate pay vouchers and the record of his capture and imprisonment near the close of that sad conflict.

Regional county histories tell a great deal about the most prominent citizens, particularly those willing to pay for the privilege of inclusion. One of my ancestors only rated half a line, but even that proved helpful since it placed him as owner of a specific section of land in 1879 when the book was published.

Some of my acquaintances possess beautifully bound genealogies that document and pay tribute to their family history. Often such a genealogy has only a remote connection to the reader, containing information primarily about persons not in the direct line. The quality of such volumes is inconsistent—some are carefully researched and documented, others slipshod. Even so, these genealogies can be valuable resources; at the very least they provide a starting place.

CHAPTER 5

IF I STUDY GEOGRAPHY, WILL I BE A BETTER GENEALOGIST?

- Various types and uses of maps, atlases, gazetteers.
- Why it's worth learning about old trails and migration patterns.
- Paying attention to changing boundary lines.
- Recommendation: maintain a place index linking specific counties, states, and countries to surnames.
- The effect of geography on a particular family.
- Tracings: the travel heritage of one man and his wife.
- How to coordinate a generational chart with a migration map.
- Preparing notebooks of research tips for a particular geographical region.
- Visits to ancestral lands.

Geography very likely played a signficant part in shaping the decisions of your ancestors. A study of today's maps may explain your own present geographical location. In this chapter, I want you to see how you can become a better genealogist by studying geography.

There are marvelous collections of maps available for study, and it is worth taking time to study atlases and gazetteers and to learn about old trails and migration patterns. It is also useful to prepare your own location index to link places and surnames. In connection with such a list, give thought to the effect of geography on the family. I recommend tracing the journeys of connecting families, marking these on a map, and relating this to history. I also suggest that you gather geographically oriented research tips and that you visit ancestral lands whenever possible.

Maps, Atlases, Gazetteers

My love for maps, atlases, and gazetteers goes back to the happy hours I spent with my grandfather, who had rarely traveled outside his county but knew the world through his reading and map study. In particular, I remember his quest for identifying his French and German heritage. A globe became one of my proud possessions, and maps have decorated my walls at home; a United States map takes up half a bulletin board in my office. I once visited a home with an attractive sun porch; the owner had placed an assortment of maps on the floor, then applied a hard finish over them, allowing persons to walk upon a decoupage of countries!

Maps

Map sources include magazines, tourist centers, bookstores, and government bodies. Plat maps show the ownership of each lot in a township; townships are divided into thirty-six sections, each one mile square. The location of a particular piece of property is usually determined by its location in a section and by the township and range numbers. Besides the landowners' names, information on plat maps can include churches, cemeteries, and schools. Topographic maps show the physical features of land; they are available from the U. S. Geological Survey or through the Public Documents Distribution Center. Land ownership maps usually cover an entire county and predate both county plat books and topographic survey maps; many were prepared after the Civil War. State, county, and city maps can be obtained from a state's department of tourism or transportation, chambers of commerce, and some county offices. Road maps are basic, readily available, and nicely detailed. Antique maps and reproductions are sold by dealers and are available for viewing in special library and museum collections and at major historical societies.

There are foreign counterparts to nearly all types of United States maps. These include road maps, atlases, and topographical and sectional maps.

Atlases

An atlas is a book of maps; often an atlas will include descriptive text, charts, illustrations, or tables. I had pondered the origin of the word *atlas*. Eventually, when I looked it up in the dictionary, I found that during the sixteenth century the Flemish cartographer Gerhardus Mercator included on the title page of his published collection of maps a picture of the mythological character named Atlas and gave his book the title *Atlas*. In early Greek mythology, Atlas was believed to have been responsible for holding up the heavens. Subsequently, many of the early collections of maps included a picture of Atlas supporting the heavens, and these became referred to as "atlases."

A variety of atlases is available and useful. I especially like to study historical atlases. Maps in these books trace history from the earliest days until the present, showing the political, economic, religious, and social changes that have occurred along with major battles, landmarks, explorations, and alliances. Old county atlases were prepared for taxation purposes and consequently gave the names of landowners and their acreage; local history and even photos were sometimes included. Collections of military maps interpret battle settings. Boundary changes become evident when one compares a series of maps for one locale. Foreign atlases have obvious value, too, and can either be purchased or located in libraries. Ancestry offers a complete collection of U.S. and European maps, atlases, and gazetteers.

Gazetteers

Gazetteers are useful in connection with maps. Alphabetically, they list the names of towns, villages, and cities, identifying a location in terms of county, parish, province, and/or state. It is important to remember that some towns have changed their names or been included in different counties, or even have disappeared completely. The gazetteer is also an excellent source for information concerning the size, location, types of industry, and government bodies located in specific areas.

Old Trails and Migration Patterns

A map showing old trails and migration routes would be an excellent addition to your research handbook. This will be particularly helpful to you as you try to follow the migrations of your colonial and early American ancestors. For example, I understand the relocation following the American Revolution of Durs Ammen and his family from Pennsylvania to Virginia when I read about the Great Valley Road.

If your ancestors traveled west across the prairies and mountains, you will want to read the diaries of other pioneers, compare the alternative trails, and examine the historical accounts that parallel your ancestors' experiences. Even though most of my family migrated only as far as Iowa, I still enjoy reading about the westward migrations. Living in Kansas City, close to where more than one trail originated, has contributed to my fascination. A recent vacation highlight was the experience of following the Santa Fe Trail, visiting museums along the way, and reading related historical material.

Have you ever had the experience of recognizing identical surnames accompanying those in your lineage from place to place? Collateral lines may appear in the public records of your ancestor's previous location. Ethnic or religious groups often moved together, even naming new communities for residences of the past. Extended families frequently migrated together in support of each other for their common benefit. I remember hearing my grandmother tell about her parents' decision to accompany the mother's extended family from Iowa to Texas in 1894. Fourteen family members arrived in Texas with no hotels or places to live, so they lived together in an old store building until their homes could be built. They built their houses in a row, and the natives of the area called their little settlement "Stringtown." Six years later, the Galveston Hurricane destroyed these homes, and all but one couple returned to Iowa. They took the first train out of that area two weeks after the flood, loading all of their remaining belongings and the horses and mules into freight cars for transport back to Iowa.

Changing Boundary Lines

Boundary line changes are not to be overlooked! Many people have looked for years in a particular county or a specific state for their ancestors with no success because they were unaware of boundary changes that placed their ancestors in a different jurisdiction. My husband's south Georgia forebears can be located in three counties over the generations, though they never moved. And his Columbia County heritage traced its roots to the parent county of Richmond. My mother's grandparents in southeast Iowa had an amusing situation right in their own home—the living room was in one county, the bedroom in another!

Obtain maps for a variety of time periods for the states in which you work. Compare these to your census work. Pay attention to the county and township listings and the occasional maps that appear in the printed census books.

Place Index

It can be very helpful to maintain a place index linking specific counties, states, and countries to surnames. The easiest way to accomplish this is through a computerized database sort, but it can be compiled in other ways, too.

Prepare a separate sheet for each state in which you work. Next, list the counties of that state in which you had family. Under a county heading, record the names and dates of each family in residence. You will find this preparation valuable when you visit an area or even when you browse the library shelves—include it in your research handbook and keep it in your travel bag.

Geography's Effects on a Particular Family

We are all curious about our immigrant ancestors. Do you ever try to imagine what their ocean crossings were like? My grandmother's research revealed that Durs Ammen had come to America from Switzerland. She had even given me a

Place Index

County	Ancestor	Timespan of Residence
Compiled By:	For State Of:	

photograph of him made from a charcoal likeness dating back to about 1780. Now, however, when I look at his portrait, I do so with the knowledge that he actually crossed the ocean not once but three times. One wonders what experiences each ocean voyage brought.

On one of my many library visits, I found a translation of Swiss records explaining that this man had returned from America in 1752 to claim an inheritance for himself and a brother. Moreover, the Swiss government gave instructions that once he had collected the inheritance and paid the ten-percent tax, he was to surrender his citizenship and "hasten his departure." Government officials were even instructed to "take care that Durs does not entice anyone to emigrate." Indeed, Durs Ammen did return to America, where he fought for Pennsylvania in the Revolutionary War, then moved on down the Great Valley Road to settle on Virginia land awarded to him for his military service. Other family members followed. His granddaughter, Catherine Harshbarger, was among them; she married John Deardorff from the other side of the mountain range. Two of Durs' sons had already married into the Deardorff family; their families had been close neighbors back in Pennsylvania, and apparently old ties survived their parallel migrations southward despite the mountain barrier.

Tracings

Use maps to trail your ancestors! When I prepare a chronological listing of the movements of a couple from place to place, I call it a *tracing*. It is my way of examining the travel heritage of one man and his wife or of several generations in the same family. Occasionally a father went to an area ahead of some of his sons; in other situations a father followed the younger generation. Or part of the family might stay at the original homestead. Sometimes a family moved in different directions. When my Thompson family left western Kansas to move to Colorado and then on to Idaho, they would never again see the daughter who left Kansas to move with her husband, William Jones, back to his home area in southeastern Iowa.

As you develop your own tracings, support them with census records, land and tax records, and other official documentation. Add details from journals, the family Bible, diaries, letters, even family legends. For a widely-traveled ancestral couple, transfer the chronology to a map specifically for this one pair, marking each stopping place with a symbol and identifying each symbol with date and location.

In the process of developing these tracings, the necessary attention to detail may alert you to something that previously had escaped you. And I guarantee that you will develop a fascination for what I call "crosspoints." I use this term to focus attention on that point in time and geography in which two families cross each other and a marriage takes place.

Tracings can be preserved for study in a variety of ways. One is to simply make a chronological list of places and dates for each of the individuals being

Tracings

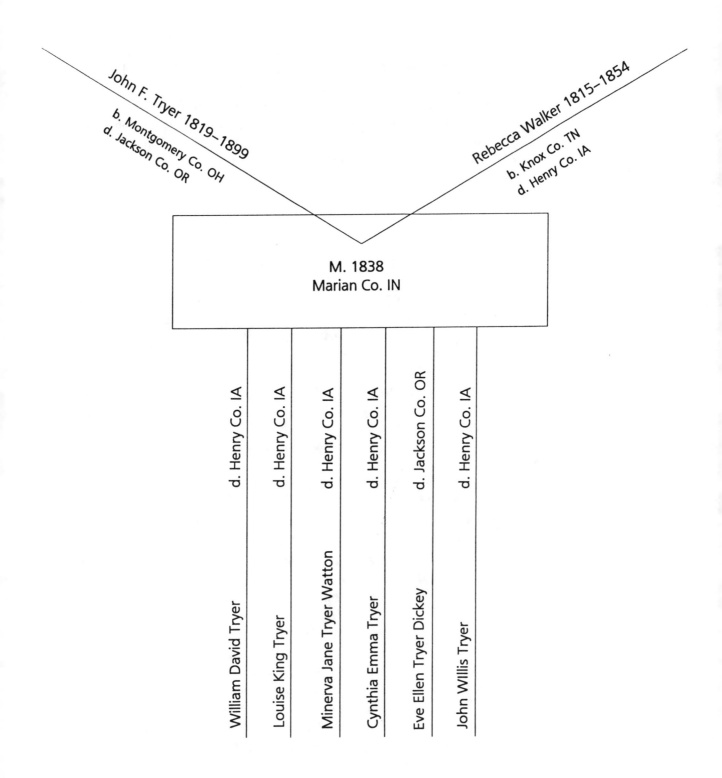

John F. Tryer 1819–1899
b. Montgomery Co. OH
d. Jackson Co. OR

Rebecca Walker 1815–1854
b. Knox Co. TN
d. Henry Co. IA

M. 1838
Marian Co. IN

William David Tryer — d. Henry Co. IA

Louise King Tryer — d. Henry Co. IA

Minerva Jane Tryer Watton — d. Henry Co. IA

Cynthia Emma Tryer — d. Henry Co. IA

Eve Ellen Tryer Dickey — d. Jackson Co. OR

John Willis Tryer — d. Henry Co. IA

compared, such as a man and his wife. Another way is to mark their journeys on a map, as already suggested. Still a third way is to chart a family in a graphic manner, beginning on the right side of a horizontal sheet with the birth of each parent, meeting diagonally at the "crosspoint" of their marriage, and then drawing lines out to the left, one for each child upon which should appear both the name and death location of each child. Featuring collateral lines in this manner can expand your research opportunities; you may find information about your ancestor by first learning about a sister or brother. Although we usually write and read from left to right, I like to use a right-to-left approach for charting tracings because the migration patterns for my family were east to west, from Europe to America and then from eastern colonies to the midwest and beyond.

Generational Migration Maps

It is startling to see how far apart some families scattered over a span of only two generations; you can see this separation on a generation map. When working on a traveling family, use two maps for the surname; mark one "Birth Places" and the other "Death Places." Next, record the locations of these events first for the parents and then individually for each child. For a complicated search, make and compare still a third map, marking the "Marriage Places." By comparing these maps, you can get a visualization of the interaction of geography and biography and begin to ponder about travel companions, the influences of migration experiences, separations, and especially the possible reasons for relocations.

As a child in southeastern Iowa, I assumed that my families had all settled there permanently once they crossed the Mississippi River. I even felt a bit disloyal moving to Missouri a few years after my marriage. Then, as I began seriously working on my genealogy, I discovered some of the older generations leaving grown children behind while they continued on westward to Kansas and Colorado, Idaho, California, and Oregon. Somehow, I had always assumed pioneers to be the younger members of a family, but this was frequently not the case.

In just two generations, my Deardorff family moved from one coast to the other, as did so many of our ancestors. Still other families spanned the oceans from one continent to another. Wars, in recent generations especially, have claimed persons far from home. Similarly, in my ancient lineage, Sir Saier de Quincy (one of England's Magna Carta sureties) died in the Holy Land as a crusader; his father-in-law, Robert de Beaumont III, was returning from the crusades when death overtook him at Durazzo, Greece.

Family Migrations
Williams—Deardorff

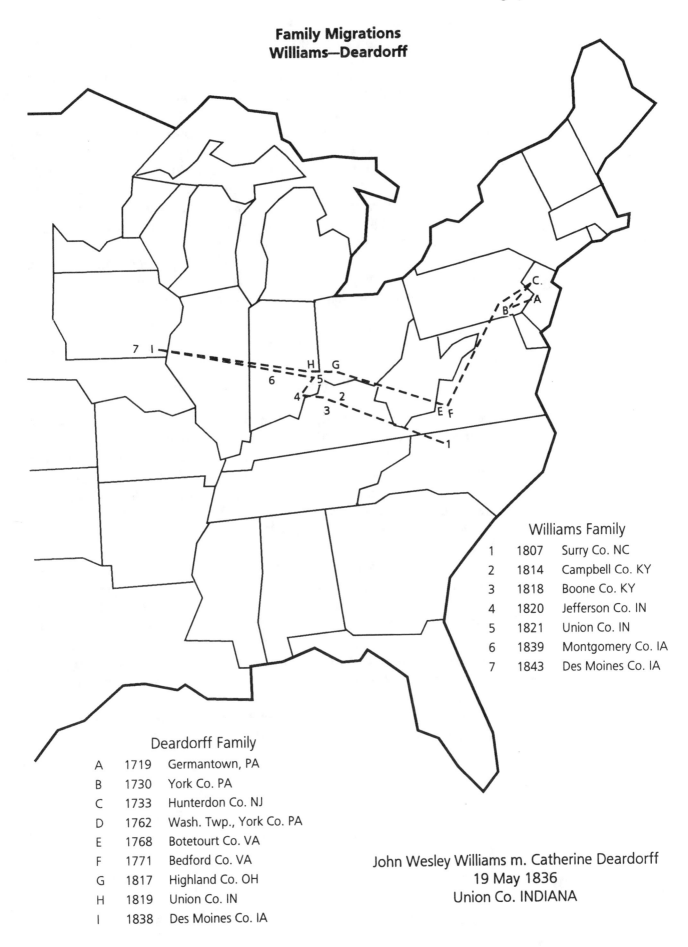

Williams Family

1	1807	Surry Co. NC
2	1814	Campbell Co. KY
3	1818	Boone Co. KY
4	1820	Jefferson Co. IN
5	1821	Union Co. IN
6	1839	Montgomery Co. IA
7	1843	Des Moines Co. IA

Deardorff Family

A	1719	Germantown, PA
B	1730	York Co. PA
C	1733	Hunterdon Co. NJ
D	1762	Wash. Twp., York Co. PA
E	1768	Botetourt Co. VA
F	1771	Bedford Co. VA
G	1817	Highland Co. OH
H	1819	Union Co. IN
I	1838	Des Moines Co. IA

John Wesley Williams m. Catherine Deardorff
19 May 1836
Union Co. INDIANA

Preparing Geographical Research Tips

You can gain a lot of insight by preparing notebooks of research tips for a particular geographical region. The bulk of my research for recent generations needs to be done in Iowa and Georgia. Consequently, I have gathered much material about how to do research in these two states. I eventually compiled these into separate notebooks, which I review before each visit. Now, as I find earlier generations, primarily in North Carolina and Virginia, I see a need to do the same for those states. Fortunately, I am in a study group that includes those two states, and I know much good resource material is readily available to me. For states that hold lesser interest for me, I drop whatever comes to my attention into a file folder for that state, knowing the time will come when I can use it. In addition, there are now some excellent guides to regional research available, both in general survey reference books and in individualized, concentrated booklets. Gradually add some of these to your bookshelf.

Visits to Ancestral Lands

Occasionally, you might read about a special tour group going to a specific area to do genealogical research. One of my more remote lines reported recently in their family newsletter about a trip to France made by a good-size group after planning at the previous summer's reunion. It was a pleasure to read about their experiences; things now seem more real to me, almost as if I had been with them. Certainly the persons on the trip must have felt closer to their ancestral fathers by covering the same ground, even locating the old family residence from two centuries ago!

Perhaps an overseas visit is beyond your budget or time allotment for travel. As an alternative, consider making a trip closer to home into an area important to your heritage. With advance planning, you can probably combine some research at courthouses, libraries, or archives in the area. You may even be able to locate distant relatives who share your interests. Or you can seek out historians of the area who may be able to answer some of your questions. For excellent tips on making the most of a research trip, see Anne Ross Balhuizen's *Searching on Location*, published by Ancestry.

Between visits, or if necessary in place of them, let your mind travel for you through reading, map study, videos, and television.

CHAPTER 6

WHO CAN HELP ME MULTIPLY MY RESEARCH EFFORTS?

- Gaining family support and participation.
- Establishing networks of "cousins."
- Chain of results accomplished through correspondence.
- Sample query formats.
- Using publications of genealogical organizations—surname, regional, historical, lineage.
- Study groups as a resource.
- Workshop leaders, class teachers, librarians, archivists, and lecturers as resources.
- Hired researchers.

Family research is not an activity for you to do exclusively on your own. Methodical review of your research, recordkeeping, and filing activities may be accomplished in isolation, but research itself involves other people. Even a homebound invalid can interact by mail, computer modem, and telephone with persons who can multiply research effort.

In this chapter I offer suggestions for gaining the support and participation of both your immediate family and a network of correspondents. I also point out how to benefit from organizations and their publications.

Are you fully utilizing the people resources available in your community? Their collective knowledge will prove invaluable to you. Moreover, new friendships are likely to develop as a marvelous side benefit.

Enlisting the Family's Support

Only rarely will everyone in a household share enthusiasm for genealogy. My husband enjoys hearing about the results of my research, but he doesn't like doing it himself. Even so, I find myself calling upon his knowledge of history, his memory for detail, and his ability to solve problems. Our oldest son, David, tolerates my hobby; our younger son, Mark, shows an occasional polite interest.

Most of our vacations in recent years have included some genealogical side trips. One year, when our boys were still quite young, my husband agreed to take them to the zoo in Atlanta while I visited the archives to do research on his families. Imagine my surprise when they were back in only two hours! I was able to extend the visit another two hours by enlisting their participation in copying entries from a card file and using the photocopier. The following year, I was granted another four hours at that archives. Several years passed and the boys were in college when I accompanied my husband to Atlanta for a business conference; this time I was able to spend two entire days at the Georgia archives! Similarly, I spent a day at Iowa's historical society building and most of the next at their local genealogical society library.

One of our favorite vacation areas has been the Great Smoky Mountains, which we often visited en route between Missouri and Georgia. One year the family agreed to journey over and around some mountains to Maryville, Tennessee, with our destination being the courthouse lawn. My Daughters of the American Revolution (DAR) magazine had included an article about the local DAR chapter establishing a monument for the Revolutionary soldiers of Blount County. Knowing that my ancestor, James Matthews, ought to be among those listed, I was eager to see this for myself. Our visit was successful, and we confirmed it with photographs that I treasure. My only regret was that our visit was poorly timed; on that Sunday afternoon it was impossible to supplement this tribute to my ancestor with a visit inside the courthouse to locate legal records. I detected no such regret in my husband and children, however!

We broke up a trip across the state of Kansas with a mid-morning visit to the Thomas County courthouse and a brief visit to Colby's public library. Even though these stops amounted to only about three hours, I left there with photocopies of homestead records, marriage and death records, maps, and news clippings.

I even managed to include several genealogical twists during a chartered bus tour through Canada and New England. From my hotel in Toronto, I made some phone calls. En route from Toronto to Ottawa, I identified the home area of my Benedict and Wing families. After a busy day of sightseeing in Boston, my husband and I set out for an evening walk down Newbury Street, which brought us to the doorstep of the New England Genealogical Society Library on the very evening it was open; our dinner was delayed by two hours!

Children or grandchildren can be involved with genealogy when they are quite young. You might consider becoming a genealogy merit badge counselor for the Boy Scouts as I have. This is one of the best ways to introduce genealogy methods to your own children and to other youth in the community. School assignments may provide another opportunity to assist a child in investigating his family heritage. My own initial family research occurred as preparation for a high school English theme; after keeping the theme for over twenty years, I began to add to it in 1976 as a way to add personal meaning to the bicentennial celebration.

Holiday gatherings are splendid times to celebrate the past. Retell the stories, bring out the traditional ornaments, prepare the recipes that have been handed down in the family, recall events from other holiday seasons, and don't forget to ask the oldest members in the extended family to tell about their childhood memories.

Parents, aunts and uncles, grandparents, cousins—you'll want to enlist them all. When you have the opportunity to visit them in their homes, comment upon any articles or photos on display that have family ties. Learn the stories that accompany them, and share whatever information you can provide to give still more meaning to such objects. Follow up your visits with letters or phone calls that refer to these and other connecting links between you, perhaps asking a few questions or seeking confirmation of details.

When a relative gives you a family heirloom, learn all you can about it, then establish it in a place of honor in your home. You will find that such objects and their stories become incorporated into family legend and, before very long, you will hear your children relating the stories to visitors.

There are expenses involved in genealogy as a hobby, and I have appreciated being able to spend conservatively and creatively to indulge my hobby. One of my friends has encouraged her husband to purchase genealogical books for her as gifts on birthdays and other special occasions, a plan which seems to please them both.

Networks of "Cousins"

Establish a network of "cousins," who collectively can search for information on a common ancestor. You will be delighted with the progress you can make when you join forces with others.

My grandfather knew the name of his great-grandfather, Jacob Thornburg of Iowa and Indiana. By answering queries and using published surname indexes for Iowa, I located half a dozen distant cousins who in turn referred me to still more and finally to a gentleman in Indiana who was just ready to publish his book on the family. By the time I "mail-met" this particular cousin, I had traced my line back ten generations and was therefore prepared to merge into his lineage for another ten!

Working cooperatively on the family's history with another family member is especially satisfying. One of my grandmothers learned to type when she was in her seventies so that she could prepare a book about her Williams and Deardorff families. In it she wrote about her unsuccessful efforts to pinpoint the marriage of Nehemiah Williams and Cynthia Ann Bowden. She had even hired a professional researcher to no avail. I worked on the problem for two more years; it was a proud moment for me to visit my grandmother to tell her how I located the missing piece of our puzzle.

Once I answered a query about a Watton family, only to discover that my new correspondent's chief suggestion was for me to write to a lady who truly is my second cousin. I came full circle also with a correspondent on the West Coast who generously shared many pages of material on two of my families—one on my father's side and one on my mother's. Imagine my surprise when I began reading correspondence from ten to fifteen years earlier—first a letter from my father's mother and then a letter from my mother's great-aunt!

My other grandmother located two real cousins out in Idaho and began an exchange of letters which in time I continued. Recently one of them sent me a photo of her grandparents—"Thought this might be of interest to you." By doing this, she introduced me to my great-great-grandparents!

You will find it interesting to identify the interrelationships of the distant cousins you meet through correspondence. A helpful gesture on your part might be to include in your letters a blank "relationship chart" with your name, that of your correspondent, and that of your common ancestor along with the names of the intervening lineages.

I keep a card file on each surname with my lineage on the first colored card, followed by individual white cards for each correspondent, for whom I list both address and their lineage. This permits a quick and accurate comparison survey for subsequent correspondence.

Chains of Correspondence

One way to initiate correspondence chains is to send a form letter (see below) and a three-generation chart of your earliest known pedigree for a particular surname in which you have a special interest and which you believe to be in common with a correspondent or several correspondents. Enclose a blank four- or five-generation chart along with an SASE, requesting that it be returned along with the names and addresses of any other persons who might have information to share.

Another way to begin a chain of correspondence is by answering a query that connects to one of your lines. Often your letter intersects with others, and a network correspondence develops. This may occur over a period of several years.

Many archives and genealogy societies allow you to leave a set of cards on file for a surname index or family exchange file. In 1979, I left a card at the Georgia Archives inquiring about my husband's great-grandfather, Valentine Stephens. Ten years later I received a letter from an archives visitor that provided me with the name of Valentine's father (J.W.P. Stephens) and a family group sheet listing the brothers and sisters. I compared this list of names with a letter I had received in 1984 (also in response to my 1979 card) and realized that I was now able to identify one of Valentine's sisters as the ancestor mentioned in that 1984 correspondence! I addressed a joint letter to both correspondents which put them into contact with one another. Subsequently, we acquired still more information from both of them including cemetery information, photos, letters from still more "cousins," maps, census abstracts, and photocopies of printed material. We have now identified descendants of three of Valentine's brothers and sisters; all three families are joining with us to determine whether the William and Mary Stevens found in the 1860 Georgia census are the grandparents. We had assumed that we would never make progress on the Stephens line since it is such a common name. How wrong we were!

We added to the Pullen and Tapley lines in south Georgia in a similar way. At a Kansas City genealogy workshop, someone saw the name Pullen on my surname list and put me in touch with one of his correspondents from Alabama, who has since worked with us researching the family in Georgia. We've now added persons in Arizona and Arkansas to the search, which seems to be taking us to Bedford County, Virginia. One of our Tapley correspondents is a probate judge in the county where my husband was born. Our first contact with her was in her official capacity when she answered our inquiry on an entirely different family. Several years later, she wrote to us saying that she had become interested in researching her family because so many people had come into the courthouse to gather details for family history. At the time, we weren't able to identify her ancestor, although we suspected there was a connection with our family. A few months later it all tied together through correspondence with another Georgia resident; he had copied my Tapley file card two years earlier at the Georgia archives and had only recently determined the relationship to the extensive research he had done on the family. Subsequent correspondence between us confirmed for all concerned that the judge's ancestor was the twin of our new correspondent's great-grandfather, both being nephews of my husband's great-great-grandfather, James Tapley. A bonus for us was that he gave us an additional two generations, taking us back to a Revolutionary War soldier.

Today's computer bulletin boards offer the genealogist an efficient and satisfying alternative and supplement to magazine queries and ordinary mail correspondence. Correspondence pays off—and it's a lot of fun, too!

Sample Form Letter to Initiate Correspondence

Date

Name
Street Address
City, State, Zip

Dear _____,

I am gathering information on the history of my _____
family. My three earliest generations are given in the chart on the
reverse side of this letter. I would like to acquire the names of the
parents of these ancestors plus any additional information concerning
location and dates of special events—including birth, marriage, and
death.

It may be that your branch of the family connects with mine. Please
record information about your family on the enclosed four-generation
chart and return it to me as soon as possible. I am also enclosing a self-
addressed stamped envelope for your convenience.

If you know of other persons who might be able to assist in this search,
I would appreciate having their names and addresses. If you are interested in the history or records of these families, I would be happy to
share material I already have.

Thank you for your assistance.

Sincerely,

Your Name
Your Address

Sample Query Formats

Query sample no.1:

> JONES: Seeking parents of Thomas Jones (1830–1900) of Ohio and
> Lee and Henry counties, IA. Sister was Sarah Jones Crane Best.
> Brother was William J. Jones. Three marriages: Anna Benedict,
> Rebecca Wilson, Sarah Lunn Wolf.

Query sample no. 2:

> DICKEY: Seeking parents of Ebenezer Dickey (1798–ca.1880), hus-
> band of Mary Eslinger. Is Ebenezer a brother to Samuel and Benjamin,
> who came to southeastern IA in 1838?

Query sample no. 3:

> WHITAKER: Seeking parents and spouse of Joshua Whitaker
> (ca.1750–1826) born in North Carolina, resident of Richmond and
> Columbia counties, Georgia, from 1793 to1826. Is he a brother to
> William and Mark Whitaker of Chester County, Penn., and Rowan
> County, N.C.?

Three-Generation Pedigree Chart

Prepared By: _____

Address: _____

Phone: _____ Date: _____

4. _____
Born _____
Married _____
Death _____
Residences _____

2. _____
Born _____
Married _____
Death _____
Residences _____

5. _____
Born _____
Death _____
Residences _____

Name of my _____

1. _____
Born _____
Married _____
Death _____
Residences _____
Spouse _____

6. _____
Born _____
Married _____
Death _____
Residences _____

3. _____
Born _____
Death _____
Residences _____

7. _____
Born _____
Death _____
Residences _____

Note that in all the above queries, the surname appears first in capital letters and the approximate life span is mentioned along with a geographical reference and the names and relationships of other known persons; states are abbreviated using postal designations. Most queries are limited to fifty words or less. Follow the guidelines of the particular publication in which the query will appear. Subscribers are frequently entitled to as many as three or four free queries per year; others are charged a fee.

Using Publications

Make use of publications from genealogical organizations—surname, regional, historical, lineage. At one time or another, I have subscribed to publications of all four types. We particularly enjoyed the Whitaker newsletter until its discontinuance. More than ten years ago my husband and I became charter members of the Augusta Genealogical Society in Georgia; its newsletter and publications have been outstanding, and we have found the organization beneficial even though we have never been present for a meeting and visited its library only once. We have subscribed to several historical magazines, particularly those dealing with military history—especially that of the Civil War. We read the lineage publications associated with our memberships in Daughters of the American Revolution, Sons of the American Revolution, and Sons of the Confederacy.

Also helpful are the more general or comprehensive journals including articles, letters, queries, resource lists, and book reviews. Back issues may be available to you at a regional genealogical library; your own public library may even have one or two. Be selective in your subscriptions, and find someone who has a different subscription with whom you can exchange copies for mutual benefit.

Maximize the time you spend with journals and periodicals by using a highlighter; or record page numbers and subjects on a self-sticking memo attached to the inside cover. Make use of the annual indexes provided by many of the publishers. Keep a tally on your research calendar to show which issues you have checked so that you don't waste time rereading. Send queries to the publications that will attract the most interested readership, and answer queries whenever possible.

Study Groups

Study groups are a satisfying resource for an exchange of information and new friendships and can be a source of motivation. Groups of this sort usually focus on a specific geographical area— perhaps one state or a cluster of three or four. In Kansas City, the Cumberland Gap Study Group has been outstanding.

Members bring in their own related materials, subscribe together to publications, invite lecturers, go together on research trips, and establish a network for telephone exchange between meetings. Perhaps best of all, these groups are supportive, rejoicing with individual successes, offering advice, and contributing appropriate experiences. Members almost always leave with an address, a new book title, a reference to check, a present of photocopies from another member, the loan of a publication for browsing, or clarification of a genealogical problem.

Persons as Resources

Genealogists tend to be persons who enjoy sharing what they have learned. No two are alike; the collective knowledge of even a small group of genealogists could fill many books. Look especially to workshop leaders, class teachers, librarians, archivists, and lecturers as resources. Such persons have spent much time, effort, and money in pursuing the subject of genealogy and have acquired either professional or paraprofessional status. Some of them specialize in a particular geographical area or type of record; others are generalists. Although they may do volunteer work for genealogical groups, they are usually salaried or on a retainer or compensated for a particular workshop or presentation. They are widely sought after and have only limited time to spend with any one person or small group. Do not impose beyond the limits of good taste, and don't put them on the spot to answer a question for which they are presently unprepared.

Hired Researchers

Usually you will want to do your own research, since otherwise you miss out on the fun of solving your own riddles and claiming successes. Besides, few other people will be as motivated as you to do a thorough job of investigation. Nevertheless, you may want to consider hiring someone to assist you in your research at some point; perhaps you need someone to work in another language or on site in a distant location; or you may want someone to use indexes or other resources unavailable to you.

Here are some guidelines to follow when hiring a researcher:

1. If you are financially able to do so, hire a certified researcher. If a person claims certification, is it by the Board for Certification of Genealogists in Washington, D.C.? This board certifies persons to research only in the United States and Canada. Approved applicants for the designation of Certified Genealogists are entitled to use the initials C.G. after their names; Certified American Lineage Specialists may use the initials C.A.L.S. following their names; Certified Genealogical Record Searchers are authorized to add the initials C.G.R.S.

2. Check with genealogical societies for references on any other person you hire to do research.

3. Agree on a fee. Fees are charged in one of two ways: either according to the amount of time spent in handling the client's work or according to a lump sum agreed on in advance for a completed project. Normally a client will also be charged for the professional's expenses for travel, certified copies of records, fees paid to clerks, photocopies, admissions, and even the cost of parking, housing, and meals if your research project takes the professional away from his usual work area.

4. Agree on the maximum amount of time or money that can be expended before a report is submitted.

5. Know what to expect in return for your fee. You are entitled to a full written report showing reference material and sources examined and cited along with the conclusions reached. This report should be of sufficient detail to prevent duplication by a later researcher should additional work be necessary in the future.

6. Realize that a professional genealogist is entitled to reimbursement for his or her time regardless of the success or failure of the research project.

7. In order to avoid duplication of research already accomplished, be sure to tell the genealogist in advance what is already known; also supply the data previously acquired.

8. Expect slower progress on large city or international research.

9. Recognize that there are limitations to be faced. A genealogist can only search available records, of which there are only a finite amount for any given ancestor. The further back you go, the fewer records are available. Most lines can be traced back only as far as about 1650, when civil and/or ecclesiastic registrations began. On the other hand, post-1900 research is also difficult due to privacy laws; few records will be obtainable in libraries that pertain to ancestors born in the United States after 1920.

10. Accept the fact that you will rarely achieve one-hundred percent proof. Most relationships are based on a combination of material and circumstantial evidence upon which conclusions can be drawn based on the preponderance of that evidence.

CHAPTER 7

WILL PHOTOGRAPHS AND MEMORABILIA EXTEND MY HERITAGE SEARCH?

- Collections that appeal to family members who might otherwise ignore their heritage.
- Methods for labeling and indexing family collections.
- Creative ways to preserve and exhibit photographs and memorabilia.
- Family interest in origins of both surnames and given names.
- Appropriate ways to enjoy heraldic arms.
- Family recipe file—a culinary heritage.
- Celebrating the present through portrait collections, certificates, documents, samplers, scrapbooks, diaries, individualized or family banners, cartoons, artwork.

In the process of "collecting" ancestors, you are likely to acquire heirlooms, photographs, letters, journals, needlework, and other items of family significance. These objects are part of your own particular heritage and consequently have worth well beyond any monetary value attached to them by antique dealers.

An emphasis on the past, however, should not cause you to neglect celebration and preservation of today's events. Recognize that you are making memories now for your children and grandchildren. Honor their accomplishments and handiwork by displaying certificates, trophies, photographs, craft items, artwork, and special souvenirs. These are the things that make your home distinctively yours. In this chapter I suggest ideas for arranging memorabilia into displays to be appreciated by you and your family.

Collections

Collections may appeal to family members who might otherwise ignore their heritage. We have a large collection of mugs, most of them related to Boy Scouting. But there are also sports mugs, special mugs for Christmas, musical mugs, mugs with sayings or illustrations, and antique shaving mugs that belonged to men in the family. Some of our tools come with a heritage: we have the wood plane that belonged to my great-great grandfather, a left-handed carpenter's rule, two types of levels, an adjustable bicycle wrench, a leather punch, a harness awl, a small wood-handled screwdriver, a hatchet, and several knives. Heirloom jewelry is a special treat for me. I wear it often and look forward to passing it on to my granddaughters someday.

Labeling and Indexing Collections

My mother enlisted my aid in labeling and indexing her collections of vases, dishes, and dolls. She numbered them by writing on self-sticking dots. We typed up corresponding descriptive lists on the computer and added to the lists as the collections grew. Included in these descriptions is the source of the item. Similarly, I am making inventory lists of special collections and artifacts in our home including quilts, needlework, books, tools, jewelry, dishes, and art objects.

Photographs and Memorabilia

My grandparents valued photographs and consequently were able to pass down quite a number to us. After visiting with one niece in California who was creating a portrait gallery for her new home, my father made copies of many photographs and distributed them to my cousins. Likewise my husband gathered several group photos and had copies made for others in the family. One of his aunts used a group photo as the basis for extracting a picture of her father, then sent it to us as a special Christmas present. Many older photographs, unfortunately deteriorated in Georgia's humidity and severe temperature conditions. One in particular was in very bad shape, but it was the only one in existence which pictured the family of my mother-in-law, so we had a restoration copy made.

I have always admired samplers and needlework of many kinds. I have framed some of my own work, but my most treasured piece is one that was passed down through the generations of my family. It is a fragile piece of Victorian amber bead-work mounted on a strip of navy satin, now framed for display in our living room. The bead-work spells out a four-line piece of poetry. It is the work of a great-great-great-grandmother, dating to about 1840/50.

My own interest in genealogy was renewed when I stumbled across my childhood button collection. A great-grandmother had entertained me on many occasions with her box of buttons, including the telling of stories represented by certain ones. She decided to fix up a special card of buttons for me, sewing them to a square of cardboard, then identifying the owner of the dress upon which that button had first appeared. In turn, I picked from among her buttons and from other button boxes those buttons I especially liked and sewed them on to heavy colored paper. Over the next twenty-five years, I would occasionally run across my little button collection. Finally, I decided to mount some into a shadow box, making them into a genealogical chart of sorts by representing the men with a decorative symbol, the women with both a button and the given name embroidered on linen. Consequently, there are buttons for Beverly, Velva, Nettie, Ionia, Alpha, Jennie, and Athalinda, daughter, mother, grandmother, two great-grandmothers, and two great-great-grandmothers. Clustered with this arrangement is another shadowbox filled with my husband's medals from high school, college, and military years. Above them is a tiny box containing a silver spoon from the graduation of my dad's mother along with a silver buckle from her mother's coat.

When I was small, I often accompanied my father to visit his grandparents, George and Pearl Britton. I clearly remember the day when great-grandmother presented me with a fragile old fan, the colors still vivid in the painting. At the same time she gave my father a photograph in which she was holding that fan. This photo of George and Pearl was taken during their courtship in 1888, on the occasion of a day spent at the county fair. Recently my father passed the photo on to me, and the two objects are now displayed together.

Much could be said about preservation of photos and memorabilia. They are fragile and valuable archives of the past, well worth preserving. Your time would be well spent reading from two or three of the many books on this subject and following the advice of professionals in this field.

Over the years, I have attended many ceremonies at which attractive certificates were awarded. Scattered around our home are quite an assortment earned by my husband, particularly in relationship to his employment and for his service to scouting. Lacking sufficient wall space to display framed certificates, we have instead gathered them into an album. As a birthday gift, I put together for him a three-ring binder of see-through vinyl pocket folders into which certificates fit nicely.

Surnames and Given Names

How many ways have you found to spell your own surname? Family historians quickly learn that the present spelling may have evolved considerably from the original. A general study of surnames is in itself an interesting hobby. Even if your family has little interest in genealogy, they are likely to have at least a mild interest in the development of their surname.

Although our oldest son, David, professes no interest in genealogy, he does take pride in both his name and family. He has been curious about the origins and variations in spelling of his surname. So he decided as a humorous exercise to program the computer to list out an organized sequence of possible and predictable spelling combinations. Eliminating some of the possibilities, he still produced twelve pages of fifty names each. He assembled them into a notebook and added two pages of reflective narrative, including these comments:

> Within every surname is a history and a heritage unique to all those who fall beneath its banner. One's name serves not only as a means of recognition, but as an emblem of one's family pride.

> One carries his name for an eternity so it commands the utmost respect and dignity. To soil one's title is to bring the foulest of impurities upon it and all that it represents.

> The Golden Rule warns to "do unto others as you would have done unto you." To insult another man's name is to bring an equal degree of retaliatory injury upon one's own title. To maintain the respect of others for one's own name thus requires an equal degree of respect for the history which lies behind their names.

> Respect can take many forms. For children, there is the constant temptation to ridicule peers on the basis of their names. Resistance to such temptation demonstrates an admiration of the dignity that every man, woman, or child holds in his or her last name.

> Insuring the proper spellings and pronunciations of others' names also displays a courtesy for others' names.

You can gradually investigate the background of the many surnames in your lineage. This study blends well with a study of heraldry, particularly when you have surnames of English derivation. Now, in the British Isles alone, there are probably over ten thousand surnames. In 1539, Henry VIII ordered that every parish should keep a record of the names of persons who were born, married, or died there; thus, a written record of surnames began. Earlier, around the coming of the Normans, names were handed down only among the noble class who had titles of land to pass to their children. But gradually surnames developed among all classes, related chiefly to parentage or clan, occupation or rank, nicknames, and places. Other nationalities made their impact on naming patterns as well.

People have always had first names, sometimes called given names or Christian names, even though many of them are inherited from pagan times, referring to the old gods of the Celts, the Anglo-Saxons, or the Scandinavians. The crusaders brought back names from the saints. During the Reformation, there was a popular wave of naming children after characters in the Old Testament, a pattern which has been repeated through the ages, particularly among families with strong ties to a religious community.

One year at Christmas, my father included among his presents to our children cards containing explanations of the history and meaning of their given names.

Observe some interesting naming patterns in your own lineage. Perhaps a mother gave her maiden name to a son as this was quite common. Certain names appear in alternate generations or in successive generations. When William and Henry appear over and over with the same surname, it becomes very difficult to determine who might be a son or if it is really a nephew. Beyond that, of course, we need to recognize that even brothers were sometimes referred to in archaic English as "cousins," adding to the confusion. This persists to a degree in the South where any relative of similar age is a cousin. Today, we have a fairly rigid expectation of the terms "junior" and the Roman numerals "II," "III," and so on; in previous centuries the designation of junior and senior might apply strictly to the age of persons with the same surname. We locate both Joshua Whitaker, Sr. and Joshua Whitaker, Jr. in the early 1800s in Columbia County, Georgia, but we had to find additional evidence to conclude that they were father and son.

Heraldry

In the broadest sense, using any pictorial badge endowed with special meaning could be considered heraldic. Usually the term refers more specifically to the granting of the coat of arms to the noble class by royalty, especially in England during the reigns of King Henry V and Queen Elizabeth I. Coats of arms are European. We are not entitled to use them unless we can prove descent and receive permission. Technically, since we are not subjects of the queen, Americans cannot be granted arms by the Royal College of Arms; however, we can be granted honorary "devisals," which appear the same.

For many years companies have capitalized upon our confusion and misunderstandings of heraldry and especially upon our vanity by offering coats of arms' reproductions for thousands of surnames. Unless you can prove you are the direct descendant of the original grantee, you should not claim anyone's coat of arms. As a matter of fact, in the strict legal sense, the grant passes only through the oldest son. Having the same surname does not transfer entitlement to the coat of arms.

Nevertheless, as family historians, there is reason to show interest in the coats of arms associated with the various surnames in one's line. It is a highly interesting subject, complex and fascinating, and well worth learning more about. Many excellent books are available on the subject.

In the early days, people made up their own arms and put shields depicting these arms on everything. In England, after about a hundred years, the king sent around a herald (census taker) who sketched and described the arms. This was the basis of the College of Heralds. After that, the king gave out arms to honor persons who helped him. The arms were often military in character, both useful and decorative, and were passed on through hereditary chains. It would be carried by all relatives and even his soldiers as identification during battle. The motto attached to the shield was composed of the words of the battle cry, yelled to scare the enemy. Later the motto carried more of a feeling of religious guidance. Gradually, the motto's intent was to guide, advise, and inspire in the way the father would have suggested. Sometimes families changed their motto and sent it to the College of Heralds for proper endorsement. In Scotland, the motto appears above the crest; in England, below the shield.

The term "coat of arms" is derived from the garment which was worn over a soldier's armor; it bore an embroidered duplication of the shield design. A more accurate term to use to describe the whole emblazonment of any heraldic bearing is "achievement." An achievement in heraldry is a complete display of arms, crest, and other accessories. The shield is the most important part since it carries the special devices or objects called charges which make that particular coat of arms distinct from any other. The shield frequently appears by itself without any other parts of an achievement. A popularization of heraldry brought about common use of the term "crest," today often used inappropriately. The crest is the top part of the coat of arms. There are many duplications of crests, but the shields are separate for each surname.

In describing the shield, the tincture (color, metal, fur) of the field is always given first. The colors or tinctures are red (gules), blue (azure), green (vert), purple (purpure) and black (sable). Some texts add dark red (sanguine) and orange (tenne). The metals are gold (or) and silver (argent). The two most important furs are ermines (white spots on black) and vair (blue and silver to represent the skins of grey squirrels). The general rule is that a color should not appear immediately on another color nor a metal on another metal.

The three positions on a shield most frequently referred to in a description of charges are the chief (top), fess (middle), and base (bottom). A divided shield is called "quartered." In the quartering, there is a special spot for each family.

The mantle represents a fur-lined cape, tattered in battle. The mantle was originally a piece of fabric attached to a knight's helmet to protect him from the heat of the sun. Today the mantle is important only to fill out the design. The supporters came very late—costumes worn by the boys who looked after the knight; they dressed in animal skins. Supporters are figures of living creatures placed at the sides of an armorial shield, appearing to support it.

Recognizing that you have no legal claim to a coat of arms, you still may wish to acknowledge the existence of one associated with your surname. Perhaps you will choose to display one or more since they are visually very appealing. After researching the blazoning (descriptions) of several arms connected to the WHITAKER family, I chose the simplest and stitched the shield in needlepoint for a coaster. Next I plan to stitch a complete coat of arms with the mantling and crest in addition to the shield. This will be a large piece of needlepoint. I have already transferred the design to graph paper with each square representing a stitch.

Enjoy collecting descriptions and depictions of the shields which are associated with your surnames. They make a colorful and romantic addition to a folder or book about a particular family. You could also make a collection of these shields into one notebook along with a synopsis of the significance of heraldry.

There are some fascinating stories to be sought out in connection with the representations on shields. A knowledge of heraldry is both enriching and entertaining.

Family Recipe File

A family recipe file makes a delightful culinary heritage. Several years ago, a good friend gave me a specially-designed cookbook binder for genealogists. It incorporated suggestions for including pictures and descriptions of relatives along with their recipes (written in their own handwriting when possible or copied onto cards to insert into place). This encouraged me to seek favorite recipes from relatives now deceased. I am glad to have these bits from the past.

Earlier one of my grandmothers had passed down a recipe for German cheese "as my great-grandmother made it." It began with cottage cheese, butter, salt, and cheese coloring. After letting it stand for three hours at one hundred degrees, it was to be turned into a heavy skillet into which heavy sweet cream would be stirred. This cheese could be stored in a well-buttered jar or bowl in a cool place for a week or ten days. It made three pounds.

Grandma also gave us her own "old farm recipe" for Neufchatel Cheese which used sweet skim milk, plus sour milk or buttermilk, one quarter of a junket tablet dissolved in half a cup cold water stirred thoroughly. Here she noted that we should not use aluminum, but should instead "borrow a granite kettle or crock." This mixture was to be set aside for twelve to fourteen hours in a warm place (about seventy-five degrees). When the clear whey rose over the surface, it could be drained. We were told to be careful not to break any more of the curd than possible and to place it in a thin cloth and drain. Next we were to open the cloth and work the dry edges into the center and drain again. Finally, we could add two tablespoons of salt to every four pounds of cheese and pack it into a buttered bowl. She also suggested that we add chopped pimentos. I wonder how often she made this, and also how she managed the seventy-five-degree temperature!

When you use recipes that are favorites in certain relative's kitchens, refer to them as Aunt Ruth's cookies, Aunt Delilah's scalloped oysters, Aunt Marna's homemade noodles, Aunt Helen's brownies, Aunt Janice's salads, or Aunt Pat's casseroles.

In addition to gathering family recipes, you'll find it interesting to collect regional and antique cookbooks.

Celebrating the Present

Celebrate the present by collecting and displaying portraits, certificates, documents, samplers, scrapbooks, diaries, individualized or family banners, cartoons, and artwork. This is your opportunity to connect the past to the present and take the family heritage on into the future! Today's celebrations become tomorrow's traditions.

In honor of the family surname, we have a "Whitaker Corner" near the telephone in our family room. There are five framed 5"-by-7" portraits on the wall—our two sons, their father, grandfather, and great-grandfather. This lineage portrait collection has attracted comments from visitors of all ages.

In still another corner of the family room, my husband and I have a collection of framed certificates and diplomas. Prior to our marriage, my husband had an entire wall of his bedroom covered with high school, college, military, and career documents. How much better it is to see these special things often than to bury them in a box in the attic.

Scrapbooks give opportunities to relive a special period, first by the effort that goes into the scrapbook, and second by the many times it is picked up and enjoyed.

For our twenty-fifth wedding anniversary, our sons put together a photo scrapbook of our marriage from their perspective. With gentle humor and clever subtitles, this treasury of words and photos honors and celebrates our years of marriage. Memories flood over us each time we pick up the album and leaf through it. Intended as a gift we could enjoy sharing with others, it has been great fun hearing the comments of both our friends and theirs.

In our home we have a lower-level hallway at the foot of a stairway; it leads between our garage/storage area and the family room. We moved into this house when our oldest child was in the second grade, the youngest still in preschool. For a year or more I left that particular wall bare while trying to decide what should fill that space appealingly. I decided to hang four individual banners onto which each person could attach memorabilia. Through the years, we have added a variety of Indian Guides and Boy Scout items, school trinkets, ribbons, awards, and pins of all sorts. Across the hall from these banners are two framed school portrait collections which show the changes in the appearance of our sons from kindergarten to high school graduation.

Cartoons, scenic photographs, a printer's drawer, shadow boxes, and art work round out our visual displays. We have a small bathroom off the family room. At times we have covered those walls with maps. More recently, during the boys' teen years, we replaced the maps with a variety of bumper stickers plus a large framed cartoon original by a newspaper cartoonist. In the living room we display a rotating collection of our own photography from vacation trips. Our sons used posters in their bedrooms, one of them even going beyond the walls with a ceiling collage! Our oldest son put his art talent to canvas and sketchbook, and gathered trophies for speech and debate contests. The theme for our younger son's room from birth until age four was "Winnie the Pooh"; I tripled the size of a two-page coloring book spread, traced the patterns onto felt, and mounted them on a piece of styrofoam 24"-by-72" for a wall mural.

The movers gave it gentle care when the family refused to leave it behind when we left St. Louis. A Christmas coloring book provided the patterns for a tree-skirt of felt cutouts and yarn embroidery, representing half a dozen Christmas carols.

When our children were preschool age, I kept a diary of the ordinary things we did, their cute little comments and actions, and milestone events. Years later, they have both enjoyed reading about themselves to supplement sparse memories of that period.

Use the creativity, talents, and interests of each person in the family to make your home represent and celebrate each personality. Collections and displays preserve special events and interests and help to combine past, present, and future.

CHAPTER 8

HOW CAN I SHARE
WHAT I'M LEARNING?

- Reasons for extending the family heritage
- Alternatives—framed charts, family trees, scrapbooks, journals, books, submissions to publications, computerized database, audiotapes, videotapes, photo collections.
- Biographical sketches, family legends, and surname summaries.
- Use of today's technology to enhance family history—personal computer, modem, digitizer, telephone, tape recorder, video camera, traditional and instant cameras, photocopier, fax machine, and microfiche and microfilm readers.

You will want to share the family anecdotes and memorabilia you locate with other family members. Now, too, is the right time to plan the passing of your heritage.

Scattered through a letter from a distant relative who was offering to exchange information were these remarks:

It is vital to me to understand the world our ancestors lived in—to me that is all a part of the genealogy, not just names and dates but REAL people . . . I too, am looking for a pretty solid picture of all the family lines. I guess I always got in trouble at home and at school for asking "WHY?" And as I get older, connection to family gets more and more important. In short, I will take anything—minute details, thoughts, area history. . . . I would also like any impressions or remembrances of our ancestors that you might have. . . . Wouldn't it be great to have a time machine?!

It is difficult and time-consuming to get one's material into attractive and accurate condition, ready to circulate. But as you polish segments into presentable form, make copies for family members, offer items for publication, or give materials to a historical society library or other appropriate archives where it will be preserved for the future, you will feel a deep sense of accomplishment. Think of the tragedy that has befallen some family historians, who through fire or storm have lost an entire collection of years of research. If for no other reason, protect your work by sharing it!

In this chapter I also suggest a variety of ways to display family memorabilia. I conclude with a challenge to you that you make good use of the opportunities you have through technology to extend your family's heritage.

Extending the Family Heritage

Years ago I saw a cartoon in which a child told her father, "People without children don't get to be ancestors!" As I pondered that remark, I realized how much I value my status as an ancestor. I also began to wonder what future generations might like to know about me and also what I might want to tell them about myself and our family. Clearly I need to take advantage of this insight and record our stories. Although the task is far from complete, I have begun to transcribe the events of our immediate family. I include both the monumental and the trivial since both contribute to what and who we are.

As our children were growing up, my husband and I took pleasure in providing them with special opportunities. We discovered that often our sons found much pleasure in some of the simplest of entertainment, and that they loved to repeat the activities which they had previously enjoyed. As in most families, we developed holiday traditions and attached meaning to favorite objects, began to acquire and add to some interesting collections, and took delight in the retelling of favorite experiences. I told a friend once that I no longer looked at a day's activity as belonging to that day alone. Rather, I was engaged in the important task of "making memories."

In one's role as "family genealogist," it is appropriate to record both the distant past and these "memories in the making." Here are some suggestions for the process of making roots for your children:

1. Organize, label, preserve, and present the momentos, photographs, and collections in your possession.

2. Write your own personal history.

3. Preserve an account of the early years of your children or your nieces and nephews.

4. Record the life histories of immediate ancestors whom you remember.

5. Gather details on more remote ancestors and prepare them into biographical sketches; annotate sources of information.

Ways of Preserving and Sharing Your Family History

You have several alternative methods for preserving your family history. Among them are framed charts and family trees, scrapbooks, journals, books, submissions to publications, computerized database, audiotapes, videotapes, and photo collections.

Visual Displays

Before genealogy claimed so much of my free time, I did considerable needlework. Having seen a wide variety of family tree samplers, I anticipated that I would one day make a very attractive one to frame. That hasn't happened...yet. Meanwhile, a nearly complete seven-generation chart is posted on a bulletin board in our family room, sharing the wall with framed diplomas and certificates that belong to my husband and me. Once for a name tag contest, I stitched a crossword puzzle of all my surnames onto a rectangle of checked gingham. It won a prize that day and has since been on display, pinned to my personal banner in the lower hallway.

Scrapbooks

Our family has quite a collection of scrapbooks from school days, travel abroad, mine and my husband's courtship days, Boy Scouting experiences, and best of all, the one our sons prepared for our twenty-fifth wedding anniversary.

Journals

I'm proud to have a journal written by my grandfather, and at times I have kept journals as have our sons. Now I'm putting bibliographical sketches and surname summaries into journal form. One challenge I have still to meet is to write a comprehensive journal of my own life and observations. Without that addition, it is likely that my descendants will know more about their remote ancestors than they will about me. I have located several books on the market which I could use to guide me in writing such a journal, but so far my interests have taken a turn towards other types of writing. I did make a start, however, when my husband and I celebrated our twenty-fifth wedding anniversary. Using a word processor, I began making journal entries and labeled the files HIS-STORY and HER-STORY. Topics included earliest memories, school days, travel, jobs, courtship and marriage, parenting, philosophy and religion, our homes, our children, and unique experiences.

Family Book

I admire those who put together and publish a book and place it in several libraries. My first problem would be choosing which family line to select for the honor. My second problem would be to decide on a format that wouldn't be too tedious—I can't get excited about confirming dates of all the descendants when my real interest is going beyond the pedigrees in order to get acquainted with my ancestors. Nevertheless, I enjoy browsing through family histories to see how they are written, and I am pleased to see some good how-to books on the market, telling how to prepare and publish a family book. So for those of you inclined in that direction, go for it! And congratulations!

I would encourage you to take any opportunity to place lineage information into a publication. Sometimes you can contribute to another person's book, an historical society newsletter, or a genealogical publication.

Computerized Database

A computerized database is nice to have, even though the data entry becomes quite tedious. There are some excellent software programs to consider for this purpose. I have even seen software lately which would allow the user to digitize photos and add recorded voices to a computer program along with connecting lines and labels. I use a commercial genealogy software, but in addition I use integrated business software word processing, database, and spreadsheet. As new software came along, I designed and tried various templates, some of which I have used extensively. Consequently, I have much data on floppy disks which is convenient for making alterations, insertions, sorts, and copies. A hard disk drive for my computer gives me efficient access. I maintain backup disk copies of my genealogical data, but I still like printed "hard" copies of this material for my files and notebooks.

Audio- and Videotapes

Many of today's families are producing audiotapes and videotapes although they have no special interest or knowledge of genealogy. For some people, however, this leads to greater interest in family history. And for those already involved with genealogy, recordings are a wonderful enhancement. How happy I am to have the voices of my children, husband, parents, and in-laws on cassette tape. Recently my father gave me a family recording made by my uncle onto a small black record disk shortly after World War II. Our wedding was recorded on reel-to-reel tape, and later transferred to cassette tape. Today's weddings are frequently videotaped. Home movies and slides of days gone by are finding their way onto videocassettes so that together with today's videotaping, many families are going to have a video heritage.

Photo Collections

Though instant cameras are fun to use, movies and videotapes recreate motion, and slides are beautiful, nothing quite replaces the still photo which can be inexpensively duplicated, enlarged, or miniaturized. Photography experts tell us that color will fade, and that we should select our favorite photos and have them printed in black and white in order to preserve the images for posterity. Remember, too, that copies of photos inserted into journals or books will make a double impact upon the reader.

Biographical Sketches

Biographical sketches may be only a few paragraphs or pages in length, but they are interesting to read, even for the people in your family who say they aren't much interested in genealogy. They go beyond mere dates and places and "flesh out" the bare skeleton. Be factual and annotate your information with either parenthetical notation or endnotes.

This is also the place to record the stories you've heard about an ancestor and enhance them with an appropriately colorful and accurate historical and regional setting. When your information is sparse or conflicting, make comments about the problems still to be resolved. State ideas and opinions, but do make it clear that these are only conjecture. Tell why you think something might be true, and how you hope to proceed to learn more. Although you may not be the one to carry it out, someone else who reads it may be able to pick up where you have stopped.

Legends

All families have their legends which have come down through oral tradition. These are difficult to substantiate, but fascinating to hear. Unless you write them down, they may be lost to the next generation. Some of the facts may not be accurate, but there always seems to be a kernel of truth around which the story is woven. Once the story is in writing and credit has been given to the appropriate sources, others may read the story and offer another version, an explanation, or confirmation that will make the story more legitimate. I'm still working on our family's legend that dates back to an ancestor's childhood in pre-Victorian England: "And he played with his cousin who lived over the garden wall and who later became the Queen." My mother remembered a conversation between her mother, grandmother, and great-aunt in which her grandmother admitted the family was related to King George, adding that her late husband didn't like to talk about it "because that king wasn't very nice." So we assumed the legend was connected to his Watton line. But recently I acquired the same story written in that great-aunt's own handwriting, crediting the legend to her mother's Tryer line, not her father's Watton line. So the search begins anew!

Surname Summaries

Surname summaries are my favorite way to consolidate information and go beyond pedigrees. These accounts are dependent upon the collection of family group charts and are clarified by four-generation pedigree charts; they incorporate the extra information gathered along the way. Here is where you will want to offer information about the development and meaning of the surname, describe or picture the associated heraldic coats of arms, locate the geographic origins, and then proceed to link the family members together in narrative style. As with biographical sketches, you need to annotate facts, and propose ways to extend the research and the lineage.

Using Technology

You can take advantage of today's technology to enhance family history. Personal computers, modems, digitizers, telephones, tape recorders, video cameras, traditional and instant cameras, photocopiers, fax machines, microfiche and microfilm readers can all be of great help.

Technology changes so rapidly that there is little point in describing the equipment for you. There are courses to take, articles to read, stores to visit, people to consult, products to try out, questions to ask, claims to prove, alternatives to consider.

Only a few years ago, many of the items on this list were unheard of. Only recently have all of them been accessible to the hobbyist. I can easily recall my first experiences with each. In 1981, I attended computer classes at the community college where I work; two years later, we purchased a home computer for our family. The college lab has given me experience with a modem and digitizer. When I was a child, we got along for quite awhile without a telephone; I was so excited when we got our first phone—I remember the number was 2093M. We've worn out a lot of cassette tape recorders, but the first one gave us the most pleasure, using it with our pre-schoolers in the early 1970s. We still don't have a video camera, but I've been taped several times, and I especially enjoyed seeing the film of a family reunion which I hadn't been able to attend. At one time the four of us in our family owned seven cameras.

I really can't imagine doing without a photocopier, although I don't have one to call my own. In connection with my employment at the college, I get materials at least weekly by fax; my reading tells me they will soon show up in many homes. I first used microfiche while attending graduate school, but my acquaintance with microfilm goes back to my adolescence, working at the city library where I occasionally had the responsibility of showing patrons how to use a machine that allowed them to read newspapers from "itty bitty" film.

Computers and Library Information
Today when I visit a library, I can still use microfilm and microfiche, but I must also be prepared to use a computerized card catalog . . . unless I've already accessed it from home via my computer modem.

I can take a lap-top computer with me to the library, courthouse, or archives. And if I'm traveling, I can even choose to take a lightweight printer with me to use at my motel room in the evening. Or I can send information back home or to someone else's computer by way of modem or fax.

At the LDS Family History Centers, I have choices to make. Should I read microfilm and microfiche or should I insert a CD ROM disk into one of their computers? If I choose the latter, I can print off selected material or copy it in one or more formats to floppy disk to take home for leisurely examination at my own computer station. At home, with a flip of the modem switch, I can join in on discussions or ask a question of other genealogists by accessing one of several genealogy bulletin boards. The leading commercial computer networks each serve the genealogy market, and there are occasional small private or club cost-free services as well. In addition to using the public bulletin boards, network subscribers can communicate with each other through private electronic mail.

Genealogists who are computerized now welcome disk magazines and books which they can read from their own monitors. Several are now appearing on floppy disks; others are available only on CD ROM. This is a relatively new market, but one that is growing. Likewise, the home computer enthusiast can choose to buy public record databases on CD ROM or recommend such purchases for their libraries.

Exchanging Information Via Computer

It has become extremely easy to exchange pedigree charts, family group sheets, and documentation via computer. Data can be moved via GEDCOM method from one person's database to that of another, even when they use different commercial software. Data can travel the mails on disk or over a telephone line via modem. One can study shared information, select portions to copy or merge with one's own database, or print off portions to carry away from a computer.

Sorting and Searching

Even if you don't have a computer of your own, you can access the power of massive data collection and rapid sorts. There are a number of commercial databases which advertise fee-based searches for specific kinds of information. Likewise, you have the opportunity to contribute your own research to such databases. Data entry time can be abbreviated by using a scanner to convert from the printed page to computer-accessible data. The possibilities for data entry, search, and retrieval seem nearly endless—an exciting prospect for family historians.

What additional technology will surface even before this century ends? Perhaps that is of less significance than for us to make good use of what we now have available. It's only been a few years since I talked our local genealogical society into offering a program on computerized genealogy. Another member went with me to the computer store to consult with the gentleman who would be our speaker. He didn't know anything about genealogy, and we didn't know anything about computers. It took more than one appointment to accomplish an interface between the disciplines! The lecture hall was filled to capacity with curious members and guests, all watching with much interest as a computer, monitor, and printer were assembled. Our speaker had programmed a family group sheet and then filled it out with my friend's data. Everyone was impressed and wanted him to print theirs out next, not understanding that data entry had to precede output. Some were disappointed and declared the computer useless to genealogists. But others who were there that day have since studied and purchased computers and effectively combined the two hobbies into one.

On the other hand, don't feel like you must have all the latest technology before you make progress in researching your family heritage. Recognize that your ancestors didn't have these gadgets; imagine life without these and other conveniences. From your pedigree, randomly pick three ancestors from different generations. Then select a geographical setting with which one or more of them was familiar. Now pretend that the four of you are sitting down together. How might you describe today's technology to them? What would they think of you and your lifestyle? Are you a credit to them? What questions would you like to ask? What advice would you seek? What would they think of each other? Even today's technology cannot provide this scenario, but it's within your ability through research and imagination to go . . . beyond pedigrees.

BIBLIOGRAPHY

Andereck, Paul A., and Richard A. Pence. *Computer Genealogy: A Guide to Research Through High Technology*. Salt Lake City: Ancestry, 1985.

Balhuizen, Anne Ross. *Searching on Location: Planning a Research Trip*. Salt Lake City: Ancestry, 1993.

Census of Pensioners for Revolutionary Services, 1840. N.p. 1841. Reprint—Baltimore: Genealogical Publishing Co., 1965.

Cerny, Johni, and Arlene Eakle. *Ancestry's Guide to Research: Case Studies in American Genealogy*. Salt Lake City: Ancestry, 1985.

Cerny, Johni, and Wendy Elliott. *The Library: A Guide to the LDS Family History Library*. Salt Lake City: Ancestry, 1988.

Cooke, Jean, et al. *History's Timeline*. London: Grisewood and Dempsey, 1981.

Eakle, Arlene, and Johni Cerny, eds. *The Source: A Guidebook of American Genealogy*. Salt Lake City: Ancestry, 1984.

Eicholz, Alice. *Ancestry's Redbook: American State, County, and Town Sources*. Rev. ed. Salt Lake City: Ancestry, 1991.

Everton, George B., Sr., ed. *The Handy Book for Genealogists*. 7th ed. Logan, Utah: The Everton Publishers, 1981.

Fletcher, William. *Recording Your Family History*. New York: Dodd, Mead, and Co., 1986.

Fox-Davies, A. C. *A Complete Guide to Heraldry*. New York: Dodge Publishing Co., 1909. Reprint—New York: Bonanza Books, 1978.

Frisch-Ripley, Karen. *Unlocking the Secrets in Old Photographs*. Salt Lake City: Ancestry, 1991.

Gouldrup, Lawrence P. *Writing the Family Narrative*. Salt Lake City: Ancestry, 1987.

Greenwood, Val D. *The Researcher's Guide to American Genealogy*. 2d ed. Baltimore: Genealogical Publishing Co., 1990.

Grun, Bernard. *The Timetables of History*. New York: Simon and Schuster, 1979.

Hanks, Patrick, and Flavia Hodges, eds. *A Dictionary of Surnames*. New York: Oxford University Press, 1988.

Harris, Maurine, and Glen Harris, eds. *Ancestry's Concise Genealogical Dictionary*. Salt Lake City: Ancestry, 1989.

Heitman, Francis Bernard. *Historical Register of Officers of the Continental Army During the War of the Revolution*. Rev. enl. ed., 1914. Reprint—Baltimore: Genealogical Publishing Co., 1967.

Kirkham, E. Kay. *A Genealogical and Historical Atlas of the United States of America*. Logan, Utah: The Everton Publishers, 1976.

Lackey, Richard S. *Cite Your Sources*. New Orleans: Polyanthos, 1980.

Map Guide to the U. S. Federal Censuses. Researched by William Thorndale and William Dollarhide. Available from Dollarhide Systems, Box 5282, Bellingham, WA 98227.

Neagles, James C. *Library of Congress: Guide to Genealogical and Historical Research*. Salt Lake City: Ancestry, 1989.

Schweitzer, George K. *Civil War Genealogy*. Knoxville, Tenn.: the author, 1982.

Shull, Wilma Sadler. *Photographing Your Heritage*. Salt Lake City: Ancestry, 1988.

Sturm, Duane, and Pat Sturm. *Video Family History*. Salt Lake City: Ancestry, 1989.

Szucs, Loretto Dennis, and Sandra Hargreaves Luebking. *The Archives: A Guide to the National Archives Field Branches*. Salt Lake City: Ancestry, 1988.

INDEX

8202

Please remember that this is a library book,
and that it belongs only temporarily to each
person who uses it. Be considerate. Do
not write in this, or any, library book.